The Countryman Animal Book

Edited by
BRUCE AND MARGARET CAMPBELL

DAVID & CHARLES : NEWTON ABBOT

0 7153 6285 2

© The Countryman 1973

Set in 11/13 point Plantin
and printed in Great Britain
by John Sherratt & Son Limited
for David & Charles (Holdings) Limited
South Devon House Newton Abbot Devon

CONTENTS

LIST OF ILLUSTRATIONS

FOREWORD

We have used 'Animals' in the title of this selection in a way that may offend some purists but which, we believe, agrees with the popular use of the word to mean the zoological class of mammals; frog and toad slip in too as four-footed vertebrates. Birds will spread their wings in a companion book, already in preparation, but reptiles, fish and the myriad invertebrates will have to wait their turn.

We have included a number of articles and notes on animals overseas, and on domestic animals, which have always loomed large in the pages of 'The Countryman', together with the nomansland of tamed wild animals. These last provide not only material for the student of behaviour, but often a most satisfying relationship. As G. E. Wells concludes the story of her rabbit Buster: 'I felt sad, for, in a much less spectacular way, I had enjoyed an experience as rewarding as Joy Adamson's with Elsa the lioness.'

Domestic animals also allow some intrusion of the human animal and his attitude, from the artifices of the 'travellers' in Charles Bowness's 'Some fine old business' to Michael Ryder's careful research 'Unravelling the evidence' of the origins and relationships of breeds of sheep.

Network research has become fashionable in recent years as a way of harnessing the immense amount of amateur energy and enthusiasm freed by an age of increasing leisure. The ornithologists and botanists were perhaps first in the field, but many people involved with natural history have now followed their lead. The setting up by the Nature Conservancy of the Biological Records Centre at the Monks Wood Experimental Station in Huntingdonshire means that no observation need now be wasted: all can be stored for posterity. But 'The Countryman' has its own network of equal age; perhaps it is not a coincidence that the first national census of heronries took place two years after the first appearance of the magazine. The same wind was blowing for both, though in our case it followed the honourable tradition of Gilbert White and his correspondents, bringing in an ever-growing supply of articles and notes on all aspects of natural history.

The vast majority of these offers do not reach the printed page. We have at no time dealt with reports of rarities as such: there are plenty of journals, national and local, in which such records are properly at home. But whenever new light is thrown on some problem of animal behaviour or valuable additional observations made in a field not yet fully explored, we try to find space. In 1969 the features 'Incidents of Bird Life' and 'Wild Life and Tame' were combined and a new feature, 'Looking at Nature', gave B.C. the chance to discuss more fully topics which appeared to interest several readers or which his own field work had turned up. Several extracts appear in this selection and are described as 'compiled by B.C.', since they almost always contain the observations of others.

But this is no scientific symposium: a number of poems express delight in animals in a variety of keys, in keeping with one great tradition of British poetry, whether in English or the Celtic languages.

The animals are arranged in alphabetical order, to make for

easy browsing here and there, as well as for continuous reading. It is chance, but appropriate, that baboons are the subject of the first article, because their social life bridges the gap between man and the animals and so introduces the tenuous theme of the whole book, the interaction between human and non-human, both as groups and individuals; that this particular episode ends in tragedy is only too frequent an outcome of these often fatal relationships.

If a vote could be taken on Britain's most popular mammal, there is little doubt that the badger would top the poll; it is the symbol both of the county conservation trust movement as a whole and in particular of the Berkshire, Buckinghamshire and Oxfordshire Naturalists' Trust, who maintain that their head is that of a boar, while the national one is a sow. Anyway, we have given badgers a good look-in, with Arthur Jollands's summary of long first-hand experience and an account of a 'badger's funeral', something that has very rarely been seen and about which melophiles would like to know more.

The short section on bats includes another overseas note and some 'field' notes on the whiskered bat, with a record of one sleeping on its side instead of the apparently obligatory upside-down position, shared also by one group of parrots.

It is hard enough to be objective about wild animals; when it comes to their tame relatives, who may be our daily companions, it is even more difficult and we have not hesitated to include notes and verses catching the spirit of the special relationships that exist between cats, dogs and their owners. Cats, in particular, stimulate the muse; dogs are more prose subjects, but who can confine Lord Dunsany's 'moment' in the second category: we are convinced by it that this is how a dog thinks.

Our stance is a little farther from cattle, whether it is V. O. Lonsdale and his team trying to negotiate with Abdul the Jersey bull, or Margaret Keech and Elaine Bullard musing on the characters of cows.

Two vivid pictures of red deer stags during the rut are included

13

in the section on deer, one in a Herefordshire park and the other in the Quantocks, where a wild stock still holds out. Phoebe Hesketh's poem could describe the first day of any fawn – roe, fallow or sika.

Dormice give Kenneth Underwood a chance to show the skill of his pen as well as his superb scraperboard technique; it would be heartening to have more good news of these once familiar and favourite little rodents.

Foxes can be relied on to unleash both poetry and prose, with Lady Braid-Taylor's account of how M & B outdid a vet's gloomy prognosis and restored sight to her pet 'Raishy'. Enoch the frog proved his worth as a pesticide, with no dangerous side effects.

Goats includes a note by Henry Tegner on the 'wild' herds that he has known for years on the Cheviots and which have counterparts in many hill areas of Britain; Paul Henry writes about an Irish herd in County Wicklow and the clash of two billies in what corresponds to the rutting season; F. G. Turnbull, elucidating the 'crimes' of the disarming Phyllis, gives more food for ethological thought.

The hares section consists mainly of Alex Tewnion's article, based on arduous first-hand field work, about one of the less known but by no means scarce British mammals, the blue or mountain hare, as studied on a hill not far from Crieff in Perthshire. Hedgehogs includes an article by another blue hare enthusiast, Raymond Hewson, who writes this time about two hedgehogs introduced into his garden to keep down 'hordes of slugs', but who soon needed their diet supplemented with raw egg and minced steak. Two notes on hedgehog courtship throw some light on a subject still remarkably obscure, while an exhibition of road sense by a mother with her young is something to offset against the many pathetic casualties which are most people's 'sightings' of this endearing animal.

Horses provides various fare from the shoeing of Mettle, 'a shire, grey and vicious', to a note on his ancestor the medieval great horse, who carried armoured knights into battle.

Mice covers several species, including the very active and successful long-tailed field mouse or wood mouse; but G. E. Young's efforts to foil raiders of peanuts put out for titmice may well have concerned the not very well known yellow-necked mouse, which is even more powerful and acrobatic than its relative. Richard Stileman's 'Moles on the farm' summarises a very neat piece of research and observation showing how compaction of the soil affects the mole's hunting efficiency.

Apparently wanton infanticide by a male monkey, so perceptively described by Bhabani Bhattacharya, in a central Indian village, makes an unusual item in a chronicle predominantly of British mammals, résuméd by a full section on otters, which must run badgers close in the popularity stakes; this includes a description by R. M. Lockley of an otter family at play somewhere in the Inner Hebrides, where many live an entirely marine life. Indeed it was a seagoing otter in the morning that made a notable double on the day we visited Sealgair's sanctuary in Wester Ross a couple of years ago, and saw for ourselves the relationship he has established with pine martens.

Herbert was a sort of ugly duckling who rose to become champion of champions among New Zealand pigs. Two Australian mammals are the subject of short notes before Joyce Averil Burgess's commensal pygmy shrews. Both these and the common shrew seem to be regular house-dwellers; we ourselves have seen one sharing the milk saucer with our old ginger cat.

So to rabbits and the lovingly told tale of Buster. Then a striking example of 'sagacity and determination' by rats – an antidote to the anthropocentric nonsense to which these enterprising aliens are usually subjected; and two contributions on seals, one epic, one playful: the fight between the bull grey seal and the giant conger on Rathlin has a symbolic quality in keeping with the island where Robert Bruce saw his spider.

The section on sheep includes Richard Perry's account of the Shetland breed, probably no longer pure, and a note from the

Reverend Richard Clough on a ram who charged his reflection in a mirror.

A longish section on squirrels reflects how large a place the grey squirrel has come to take in the observations of readers, because of its diurnal habits and inquisitive, not to say acquisitive, behaviour. Robert Gillmor's drawing epitomises their attraction, and no doubt we shall continue to walk the emotional knife-edge between condemning them, rabbits, rats and mice as pests in the mass and fraternising with them as individuals.

Stoats and weasels are the two most frequently seen British carnivores, and there seems no end to their traits of behaviour: climbing walls, 'rolling' rabbits, raiding bird tables, hunting communally in mid-winter, and 'shamming' dead, possibly as the result of a parasite in the skull – surely as strange as anything conjured up about Irish 'witherets'? Interposed between these two active predators are a televisionary toad and a short discussion on water voles, those charming and innocent inhabitants of the riverside, whom Kenneth Grahame immortalised but Beatrix Potter seems to have ignored.

A short paragraph on a wild cat in Sutherland reflects the extreme scarcity of first-hand observations on this rare mammal, now more numerous than for a century and a half and a possible invader of Northern England.

The book ends with two articles, one about real, the other about pseudo-Africa. Charlotte Truepeney, author of 'Dear Monkey' and 'Our African Farm', mates her evocative prose with delicate sketches of wild life in the Gorongosa Reserve: B.C. more prosaically reviews the growth of safari parks in late twentieth-century Britain.

Finally there are the illustrations; no doubt many readers will turn to these first and, we hope, find in them that blend of the *chose vue* tellingly composed and of high technical quality which distinguishes 'The Countryman''s photographers. Kenneth Underwood's scraperboards need no encomium: they are some of the most exciting to come our way for years.

Bruce and Margaret Campbell

16

BABOONS

Four on a Mountain by P. J. le Riche

The four baboons were permanent residents, I found. My work as a geologist had not previously brought me into the deep country in South Africa, and my new neighbours interested me. They ranged widely during the day, foraging, but late afternoon always found them back on the mountain, seated on a large rock, facing away from one another with a rigid immobility that was impressive. I decided that they were a sage old male and the remnants of his harem, survivors probably of a once numerous herd. This theory was upset by the discovery that they were all males. An alternative one, that they were a band of brothers who had withdrawn from their world for the sake of contemplation and the enjoyment of one another's society, did not stand up when I found that, if two so much as bumped into each other, snarls of rage tore the peace of the day to shreds and, as often as not, a fight ensued. They foamed at the mouth and displayed fangs inches in length.

Yet there never appeared to be much damage done, to my amazement. They were pulling their bites, I concluded; their place was in the Johannesburg wrestling ring. Born showmen and actors, they would be appreciated there. 'But you don't get away with it with me,' I shouted to two who had staged an evening brawl.

One afternoon, when the sun was still high, two of them began a fight. It was a more than usually noisy and apparently savage affair, and I walked up to meet the combatants, who were banging their way among the rocks down towards my camp. They were taking no planned course, but were occupied solely in inflicting injury on each other, and gravity was doing the rest. I took my stance on a rock a little out of their course, and watched the fight approach, with some amusement and an odd feeling that something was wrong. Frustration was in every roar and snarl, and yet they were at close enough grips and appeared to secure dangerous enough bites to satisfy any bloodlust. The fight raged past me, and a few yards below an unusually hard bang against a rock separated the combatants. Each lay where he had fallen, too exhausted to move.

After viewing the spectacle not unsympathetically, I began to find it funny and ultimately laughed heartily. On this the baboons sat up and eyed me malevolently. From their shallow, inordinately close-set, earth-coloured eyes they directed glances at me that spoke of pure, untempered hatred and malice. Their ill wishes were so concentrated and stark that for a moment I felt a chill of misgiving, but again their unmixed hatred and utter lack of dignity and reserve got the better of me and I laughed. This time they did not look at me, but rose painfully and struggled up the mountain.

The baboons continued to puzzle me, and I wrote about them to a friend: 'I have for neighbours four old baboons who appear to have renounced their world. That was what I had concluded, but something happened yesterday that suggests a different explanation. In the morning the quiet of this place was suddenly invaded. It gave an uncommon vivacity to the scene and stirred even me with a suggestion of fuller life. You know how one responds to a crowd after a spell of loneliness.

'I had climbed over the mountain, passing close by my four neighbours, who have accepted me as part of the scenery. They take little notice of me except to bawl, now and again, something that has an insulting inflection.

'I was below the western ridge of the mountain when I became aware of a multitudinous life approaching from the west, and there burst into view a herd of baboons of all ages and sizes and temperaments apparently. They passed within a hundred yards, and some wandered within twenty, without detecting me, as I had taken cover. They were a lively, busy set, and their social life lay fully exposed. Stones were lifted, and scorpions and other creeping unfortunates extracted. Being no lover of scorpions, I was fascinated by the casual way the sting of one would be nipped off, without its being deigned a glance, and the absent-minded way in which the body would then be rubbed on the ground to stun its activity before it was transferred to the pouch in the cheek.

'Children were thrashed for misdemeanours I sometimes detected and sometimes did not. It struck me that some parents were readier with slaps than others. I saw a lover and his lass reach complete understanding, while a rival sat by and made the best of it. He did not really make a better job of it than you or I would have done.

'Then there was an abrupt silence and a tenseness among the crowd, and for a moment I thought they had discovered me; but, hearing excited yells and roars behind me, I scouted in that direction and saw my four old friends galloping up. Their intentions were obviously peaceful; their emotions those of the wanderer returning home. I make no pretence of understanding their language, but I knew as plainly as though I heard you shouting it that they were calling to one another: "Back to civilisation, boys". It was the only time I had not sensed an acrid hostility between them.

'But, alas! It was the tooth of civilisation that met them, not its glittering prizes. They were met by four males of the tribe, and a fight as ferocious as those they have among themselves ensued, and on their part it was as ineffective. I cannot understand this, as they are physically able and their teeth terrible to look at. If it was ineffective on their part, however, it was not so on that of their opponents, and in a few moments, torn, battered and bleeding, they were dragging themselves away.

'I stood up and shouted, "What a damned shame!" I felt like one of the tribe, and a moment later would have called an indignation meeting, but my appearance caused as much consternation as the Devil's would at a children's party. Youngsters sprang to their mothers' backs and clung to their bellies, shrill cries rent the air, hoarse imprecations thundered past my ears, and so sudden was the retreat that a part of the mountain-side appeared to have melted away.

'My four old friends dragged themselves about miserably for several days, but are now recovered and average about two fights a day, for which I am thankful for their sakes, because without these fights the monotony of their existence would be dreadful. Theirs is a hard lot, and their loyalty to what, I suppose, is tradition makes it a difficult one to improve.

'The nights are often bitterly cold, incredibly so when compared with the heat of the days, and the baboons have no shelter. The frost deposits on their coats. When the morning sun restores the circulation and their blood painfully finds its full course again, they give loud and unrestrained yells, grasping each afflicted limb in turn with the other three, self-pity supreme in their minds until the pain is gone, when bad temper immediately takes its place.

'I built them a shelter while they were out foraging, but they don't spend the nights in it, although they gave it a thorough inspection. Each takes one side to lean his back against. The result is that, as they do not see so much of one another as formerly, fights are becoming less frequent. On extra cold nights I have gone towards their place and heard the chattering of their teeth. I built a fire near them, hoping that when I had gone they would come and sit round it, relax and tell lies like reasonable people. But they will have none of it, and it seems to be a point of honour with them now to pretend I don't exist.

'In the herds, I have been told, they keep warm by huddling together. I can't see these four in any embrace but a mortal one, for they hate one another with a fine, rare quintessence of the quality from which no kindly drop of tolerance could be wrung. Then why do they keep together? You tell me.'

One morning I was awakened by the sound of a rifle shot. It was followed by two more before I arrived outside the tent, to see the last of the baboons trying to escape. The numbing terror that often overtakes baboons when in danger had slowed his movements to a grotesque slow motion. As I saw him he seemed to fold in. There was a thud, like that of a hanging carpet being struck, and then followed the sharp report of the rifle. By that time the baboon was dead.

I watched the tall figure of the farmer approaching with the rifle under his arm. He saw that I was angry, and to him there seemed to be only one explanation for that and he hastened to defend himself. 'No bullet passed within a hundred yards of your place,' he protested; 'and I made sure there was nothing in the line of fire'. 'I am not angry because your bullets passed too near,' I said. 'Why did you shoot the baboons?' 'But,' said the farmer, 'you always shoot a baboon. Except a tame one, of course – one tied to a pole or in a cage, you know,' he went on, wishing to make everything quite clear. 'Unless, of course, you can ride him down and hit him over the head with a stirrup iron, which saves a bullet,' he continued, still with the idea of exposing all the hidden aspects of the problem.

The farmer looked me over and began to realise that what was obvious to him might not be to me. 'They got among some lambing ewes of mine, yesterday,' he said, 'and tore open several lambs. The shepherd told me it was this lot. So I came to make an end of them.' 'Tore open the lambs! Why?' 'To get the curdled milk in their stomachs. They have a weakness for that.' 'Dreadful!' I said. 'No. Just animal nature. They go for what is easy, especially if they like it.'

I walked over to the nearest baboon and, lifting its lip, looked with astonishment at the terrific fang exposed. It was longer than a lion's – twice the length. Then I heard a chuckle behind me. 'Looking at his teeth?' the farmer asked. 'They look terrible, don't they? Well, they are harmless. Look.' He stopped and took hold of the jaws of the baboon. 'No matter how far apart I pull them, the points of the upper and lower canines don't pass one another. They have grown too long. I don't know why it happens – wrong food perhaps. When they get like this, the younger males drive them out of the herd. This old fellow's tearing teeth were useless to him. He could only pinch with his front teeth, and he couldn't get much into his mouth.'

The farmer fingered a gold-mounted tooth, absent-mindedly, in his own upper jaw: 'I have always been thankful they improved on nature to the extent of inventing dentists.' He considered. 'Just teeth are not enough,' he said.

BADGERS

A Family of Badgers by Margaret Pickersgill

One evening about Whitsun I was returning down a small ghyll in Airedale, when something moved off quickly on my left. I hurried up the steep bank and caught sight of a creature moving slowly backwards, humping its back as it went. When I came within about thirty yards of it, I saw that it was a large dog badger drawing dry leaves and grass backwards by a series of jerks with his chin. His mate was there to guide him; she kept going a little ahead down the track and then returning. Not until I was within about fifteen yards of them did they pause and take a few steps towards me - more out of curiosity, it seemed, than in anger, as though they had had no previous contact with a human being. I stopped and they resumed the job in hand, squeezing under a wire fence and passing into the wood which lines that side of the ghyll. Twenty yards inside the wood they vanished. It was too dark to see the mouth of the set plainly and I was left wondering whether they were going to have cubs as late as June.

On the next evening I was there at dusk, and after a long wait I saw the striped face of the dog badger at the mouth of the set. He lifted his nose this way and that, then put his forepaws up on the ground over the back of the hole and sniffed again. Evidently he was not satisfied, for he retired out of sight and did not re-appear.

It was August Bank Holiday before I was able to visit the spot again, and then I tried a different approach, through a field at the back of the wood, against the wind. The two mouths of the set were only ten yards from a low wall which bordered the wood, and the badgers' usual path came even closer to the wall. My eyes soon became accustomed to the darkness of the wood and I had just time to wonder whether the noisy departure of a wood-pigeon would warn the badgers of my presence, when a cub put out its nose, gave a cursory sniff and came into the open. It was followed immediately by two more cubs. The first one ran up the path and seized a stick which it tossed into the air; the others dashed after it and a playful scrap ensued. They mauled one another with their teeth like puppies, rolling over and over. Then one would break away and rush down one entrance to the set, only to appear a moment later at the other. Sometimes they would chase one another round a tree, or try to butt one another down the steep bank. They seemed to have no fear. Once a cub ran so near to the wall, just where I was leaning, that I could have touched it. Night after night I watched the fun, and I got to know almost to the minute when they would appear. If I was a little late, I heard them yelping and growling as I approached, and knew that I should see their frolics in full swing.

Unfortunately, as winter approached the old dog badger was accused of having raided neighbouring poultry. The hen hut was just at the foot of the bank where he lived, and it would not have been surprising if he had been tempted, but a fox which shared the set may well have been the culprit. Vengeance followed swiftly. Two of the cubs had been shot earlier in the autumn, and now men came with dogs, spades and guns. The old dog badger was killed after a tussle; but the passages of the set were so deep that it was impossible to dig out the female, or to drive her out with a dog.

The next year she mated earlier and had four cubs; but gone was their abandon of the previous year. I was able sometimes to watch the cubs at play, but could never tell when they would appear. This did not surprise me when I learned that it was a regular pastime of some of the village lads to go there in the evening with a gun. At intervals, too, they sent a dog down the set. Badgers can defend themselves against dogs, but against lurking humans they stand less chance.

Home and Dry   by Edward J. Bartlett

The summer and autumn of 1968 proved to be wetter than normal, and the colony of badgers were hard put to find enough dry nesting material. They live in a set in a high escarpment along the eastern boundary of a wood with a generally low ground level. The bedding trail led from the set, down the bank, to the wet floor of the wood; and I followed the narrow track into the field which forms its western boundary. The farmer had cut this for hay, and there the badgers had found their bedding. I carefully strode out the distance: it was 280 yards. The route taken for this marathon feat ran from the field into the wood, down through beech trees into a massive clump of rhododendrons and out the other side, towards a narrow concrete footbridge spanning a fast-flowing stream. Wet soggy leaves lay on the bridge, but a neat groove about a foot wide had been cut through them; wisps of hay along each side showed clearly where Brock had gone. The trail then led through a clump of bamboos and home up the very steep bank. One of the bundles had been conveniently left outside the set. It was bone dry, even after being carried all that way across the wet woodland floor, in reverse and in darkness.

Badgers' Habits   by Arthur W. Jollands

After I had studied the habits of badgers for many years, I started three years ago to keep notes on observations at some twenty sets at Warnford in the Meon Valley in Hampshire, and at Elmbridge in south-west Surrey. These have shown clearly that badgers have their idiosyncrasies. Some, for example, are deeply suspicious of man; but after I had paid a few regular visits to the sets of others, a movement, whistle or even clap of the hands was needed to send them scuttling back underground. In fact their curiosity increases, once they are used to the scent of man without the accompaniment of danger. On at least two separate occasions a badger has ranged within a yard of my canvas seat (which incidentally is always on the ground) and has stood there for several minutes bowing and sniffing, and also curiously looking me straight in the eye. If I kept quite still, it went confidently about its business, leaving me to mine. Such behaviour, of course, is exceptional.

On the other hand, badgers are frequently heard below ground and yet do not emerge. Hours may pass, and the observer may go on his way concerned and curious to know why his mission has proved unsuccessful. The direction of the wind is important, especially if the set has been visited only a few times, for wind carries scent as well as sound. If the set is well ventilated, as it will be if there are several entrance holes, scent is easily carried down it. This is one of the main, though least suspected, reasons for delayed emergence. At one set in a small dell at Warnford I found it quite impossible to watch the occupants successfully, though I could always hear them clearly and sometimes caught just a glimpse of them. From their behaviour the dell must have been rank with human scent, the mouth of the set being so enclosed that there was not a sufficient current of air to carry it away.

Generally I have found that badgers venture forth with such regularity that I have been able to forecast accurately, within five or ten minutes, when the first would appear at the entrance to its set, cautiously sniffing and listening for possible danger. From one of the seventeen sets which I visited in turn in the Meon Valley the occupants seemed never to emerge until the last train for the day (9.18 p.m.) had passed five hundred yards or more from the entrance, causing the ground to vibrate strongly. I learned that these badgers would almost certainly be out by 9.30. They seemed to wait for the train, because there was movement underground almost before the noise of it had died away. At Elmbridge the first evening hoot of the tawny owl appeared to bring one set to life; and a cock pheasant going up to roost every night near by,

Badger, a scraperboard by Kenneth Underwood

with the usual repeated 'chuck 'em up,' seemed to act as a signal for the inmates of a set at Warnford.

This suggests that some badgers may listen for certain sounds on waking, realising the regularity of their occurrence, and become almost dependent on them, as we might on an alarm clock. In open country badgers normally remain below ground considerably later than in cover of trees and bushes. Nevertheless, at one set which I visit on a high open hill, well away from human habitations, a badger emerged as the sun began to set after a hot summer day. The cause of this exceptionally early appearance was probably thirst, for the animal made a line for the stream at the foot of the hill; when it saw me, it retraced its steps in a flash

During one of my vigils at Elmbridge a fox came out of a hole a few yards away and wandered straight off into the darkness. Twenty minutes later a badger ventured from the same hole. Families of fox and badger cubs were being reared in the set and were often to be seen playing outside at the same time, but the badgers usually kept to one end of this ten-holed set and the foxes to the other. Badgers frequently share their homes with other animals. On the South Downs in Sussex, about 1940, four gin traps had been placed about a yard down the only entrance to an occupied set, and the next morning three of them contained live wild polecats, each weighing 3-4 lb. I did not know that there were any of these animals left in Sussex, but a Brighton furrier confirmed their identity.

I have often heard that badgers put their bedding out to air, but none has ever advertised its presence to me in this manner. Perhaps it occurs only if the set is in an exceptionally damp situation. If I were to find the bedding outside I would expect the set to be temporarily unoccupied. But the complete bedding is changed regularly at least twice or three times a year.

I have known of tame badgers being released, out of pity, up to fifteen miles from their owners' homes in the evening, only to be found back on their doorsteps the following morning. A Sussex farmer who was leaving the district took his tame badger more than twelve miles away. He always left the back door of his house open at night, so that the cowman could get into the dairy in the morning. The next day he was awakened by persistent scratching on his bedroom door, and when he opened it, in came the badger and jumped on the bed. Eventually he left the animal with his next-door neighbour, and shortly afterwards it dug a large hole in the garden under a box hedge, where it later gave birth to cubs. In the interval it had gone off and must have mated with a wild badger. The family were given full protection and remained in the garden, using the same set. This is surely evidence of strong attachment to kind and understanding people. If territory were the principal attraction, badgers would not leave so readily when they are not well treated.

The badger will not kill for the sake of killing and is peace-loving among other wild animals, except to satisfy its momentary appetite. Its diet is so mixed that it needs little of a particular food, and consequently its kills are few compared with those of the fox and other mainly carnivorous animals. The badger forages for its food in preference to hunting it, picking up anything tasty that comes its way. Incidentally, it will not touch carrion of any kind.

That some badgers do occasionally kill poultry cannot be disputed, but this is a comparatively rare idiosyncrasy. At Alton a farmer-friend of mine has a well-established set within a hundred and fifty yards of his house and building. Badgers have often been seen in the early evening and on moonlit nights in his farmyard, where chickens and geese have the run of the place, but he has not suffered any losses. For some weeks a badger regularly visited empty molasses drums that lay on their sides under an old caravan in the yard. A large cat used to resent the intruder and fly at it, clawing its back as it licked the remains of the treacle. In the end the cat lost one of its forepaws in the jaws of the badger, which did not however take advantage of its many opportunities to kill the cat.

Badger's Funeral   by Fred Dean

After three uneventful nights in a hide built in some stout branches directly over a set, we heard, late on the fourth night, a slight scratching noise on our right. As my eyes became accustomed to the new ground, I saw a strange grey mass moving inch by inch out of one of the larger holes. It was a dead boar badger being pushed out by its mate. As the carcase cleared the many sticks and stones in front of the set, it began to roll down the slope, gaining speed on its own momentum, and eventually came to rest between two moss-covered boulders. The sow, which had been watching it roll, was now standing motionless, listening. Then she shook herself, turned and vanished down the hole. In a few minutes she reappeared, pushing before her a mass of bedding which she scattered down the slope, then rushing back for more. After five such journeys, she went down to scratch a pile over her dead partner, completely burying the carcase and the two boulders. The final

A badger by Robert Gillmor

covering was of loose earth, sand and stones. Then she walked round a few times, tidied the place up a bit, patted the mound here and there to give solidity to the covering, and wandered off into the night.

BATS

Batting Records compiled by B.C.

In Winter 1967 we published a note from Evelyn Scott Brown, who watched rather more than ninety pipistrelles fly one after the other from under shingles on the wall of a house in Devon on a summer's evening. Commenting on this, Michael Blackmore said that colonies of up to 300 individuals might form in summer and usually dispersed after the young could fly in July. This figure was based on his own observations in Britain over nearly forty years. Recently we heard from H. J. Dickman that some years ago in August he counted 550 bats 'tumbling from a small hole in a fascia board' on an old farmhouse in Pembrokeshire. His innings ended when bad light stopped counting; 'how many were still inside will never be known,' he added. Consulted again, Michael Blackmore topped this score with 561 pipistrelles counted by the occupant as they left the roof of a house at Charlton Marshall near Blandford in Dorset on

Noctule bat by Robert Gillmor

25 July 1967. R. E. Stebbings was asked to advise on the removal of the colony and, soon afterwards, netted 429 bats in eleven days, publishing the record in the 'Journal of Mammalogy' for September 1968. Michael Blackmore considers that, while such numbers are 'certainly exceptional in Britain', they might be quite usual on the Continent where bats are more numerous; and he adds the uncorroborated figure of 2000 long-eared bats said to have been found in 1931 under the roof of a village school in Co. Monaghan. K. L. Jones counted 275 bats of unknown species leaving the roof of a cottage about a hundred yards from the river Usk in Breconshire on a June evening, and K. L. W. Perry recalls his experiences at Domasi in Malawi in 1964. One evening, approaching the small maternity hospital, which was of brick with a corrugated iron roof, he and his wife heard 'a tremendous drumming sound coming from the roof. It was deafening, even frightening in its intensity and we were completely baffled by it. Suddenly the noise stopped and there was an utter silence. A few seconds later a great cloud of bats flew out of the apex of the roof. Their exit into the somewhat failing light was so rapid that it was impossible to count them even roughly. They dispersed as suddenly as they had appeared, and we were still standing a little awe-struck, when a second exodus took place and another great mass of bats flew swishing up into the sky. Altogether there must have been, at a conservative guess, more than a thousand sleeping in the hospital roof'. Huge numbers have been filmed leaving desert caves in America, but this was the score from a single small building. The drumming sound, followed by a momentary silence, reminds me of the crescendo of chatter and sudden break before a flock of starlings leaves a pre-roost tree. The Perrys did not identify the species of bat, but this is not surprising. Few people can distinguish our own dozen kinds, unless in the hand, though the electronic bat-detector will separate the more distinctive voices in the field.

31

The Whiskered Bats of Jug Holes   by A. L. Pill

In Jug Holes Cave in Masson Hill, near Matlock, there is an all-male colony of whiskered bats, whose favourite roosting places are cavities in the roof and along the walls of a chamber some distance from the entrance. To reach them, the bats must fly down a twenty-foot vertical shaft and along a series of low passages. The temperature of the chamber is about 46°F. all the year round. The humidity is much lower there than elsewhere in the cave, but the walls and roof are often very damp, so that the long, soft fur of the bats is matted.

In general, the whiskered bat closely resembles the pipistrelle, from which it is indistinguishable on the wing. It is a light chestnut in colour. Its ears, when laid forward, extend about an eighth of an inch beyond the nose, and are longer and narrower than those of the pipistrelle. It gets its name from the moustache-like growth of silky hairs which extend to the upper lip. A mature specimen has a wing-span of about nine inches and, after the pipistrelle, it is our smallest native bat.

At times I have observed clusters of upwards of a dozen in the cave, but these are invariably outnumbered by the isolated specimens whose presence is more difficult to detect in the subdued light that must be used in order to avoid disturbing them unduly. Sometimes, when I have stood under a number of bats and blown gently or whistled, they have performed a concerted knee-bend movement which has entertained spectators; these people have been amused also by the grimaces caused by the arrival on my up-turned face of the parasites that infest the fur of the bats.

Contrary to general belief, the bats do not, apparently, always sleep with the head hanging downwards. The entrances to the cavities are invariably smaller than their internal diameters, so that circular platforms are formed. One April I found a bat lying on one of these platforms with folded wings, asleep on its side. No injuries were visible and, after being awakened, it allowed itself to be replaced.

The strength of the colony varies from time to time, and has

Badger at drinking place

The birdwatcher

never been known to exceed five or six dozen. Thus the rate of mortality appears to be high, even allowing for an occasional migrant, and the bats are probably preyed on by owls, kestrels and other carnivorous birds. At intervals they make a wholesale exodus. Some of these disappearances are so erratic that I have termed them 'terror flights', for they seem to occur most frequently in the days that follow the handling of the bats to determine their sex, development and other characteristics. It is remarkable how one may be detached from its sleeping place without waking up for several minutes, while another at its side will, at the first touch, set the cavern echoing with its piercing shrieks. When a cluster is approached, one or two light sleepers usually peel off silently after a few seconds; the rest remain to all appearances soundly asleep, but will have disappeared, too, if one goes away and returns a few minutes later.

An exodus is not always due to disturbance, and it is thought that there must be, somewhere in the vicinity, a colony of females which is visited periodically – perhaps not more than twice a year – by the males from Jug Holes. They have been known to be absent for a month or more on occasion. On their return to the halls of celibacy, they are accompanied by the male progeny of their previous mating.

The whiskered bat seems to develop rapidly, reaching maturity within a year of birth; the young, which may not be more than six months old at the time of their entry into the all-male lodge, are practically indistinguishable from their parents, apart from their slightly smaller wing-span and lighter fur. The average weight of a male is little more than four grams (one-sixth of an ounce), some of the newcomers being actually heavier than their elders. When I have taken specimens out into the daylight and they have recovered from their torpor, they have flown back unhesitatingly in the direction of the cave-mouth. Crouched in the semi-darkness of the entrance, I have witnessed some remarkable displays of aerobatics, as bats similarly released have sought to avoid obstacles laid across their usual line of flight.

Hibernation appears to be only partial. Even in February the bats are pretty lively and awaken at the slightest provocation. In the late afternoon of a mild winter's day they will emerge from the cave and return within the hour; whether they make further excursions at night is not yet established.

CATS

The Cats' Heaven   by L. F. Ramsey

Cats do not idly waste their day
In contemplation of decay.
They live spontaneously and so
Are happy in the world they know.
Eternity, cats say, is here
When perfect love casts out all fear.
Cats lead a secret life, content
In certainty of nourishment.
However far cats choose to roam
They know they'll find a welcome home.
Cats have their pressing love affairs
Secure from pert remarks or stares.
Cats do not have religious doubts:
Do not indulge in drunken bouts,
Nor do they ever need to lie,
They have no consciences, that's why.
Beauty is theirs in perfect poise,
Their movements graceful, without noise.
Cats need not paint their nails bright red,
They claw their enemies instead.
The household dogs they tolerate,
All others they despise and hate.
Love, grace and charm their whole lives through—
Cats have all these and Heaven too.

Cats Will Play   by Frances Williams

Cats were ever a part of our family life, always neutered and called Tommy. Mother's last, a beautiful white one, ruled the household. At night he stayed in his armchair until the fire went cold, then wandered upstairs to rattle the handle of the bedroom door. He slept on the foot of Mother's bed. At first light he cried for the window to be opened. Later he came in for a meal and a snooze. Every morning at about ten o'clock a large ginger tom appeared on the window-sill. 'Tommy,' my mother would say, 'here's Ginger come to play with you.' The pair of them dashed up to the attic, and for about an hour there was an awful din. Then two exhausted but happy cats came down for a drink of milk. Once Mother took me up to the attic after one of these romps. What chaos! Screwed up pieces of paper, bits of wool and oddments were scattered all round the room. Mother patiently swept them into a corner ready for the next playtime.

Kitten's Creche   by E. Ann Howes

A friend's cat produced one kitten in the potting shed about a hundred yards from the house. As a rule she would not let it out of her sight, but whenever she wanted a night out she would meow at the back door, march in with the kitten and wait until it was comfortably settled on lap or cushion. Then she would demand to be let out again, returning early next morning to collect the kitten and carry it back to the shed.

The Cat   by G. J. Blundell

> The black cat night, with lissom figure curled
> Upon the half-moon basket of our world,
> In momentary wakefulness first lies;
> Then lids with cloud her golden, star bright eyes.

HYBRID TALE

Five-year-old, reporting important event: 'The dairy cat has five kittens, three Friesians and two Jerseys.'

Anonymous   by William Angus

I call my cat Anonymous.
He is the most discreetest puss,
The most secretive, neatest puss,
    And always has been so.
He never tells me where he goes,
Or what he knows, but leads and shows
His needs, then sits with tail-wrapped toes—
    Mi domine Ano!
But when he condescends to play
He's called Anon or Mousecadet
Or Anna-whom-three-realms-obey
    Or just Hey Nonny No.
He has his way; there is no fuss.
His name is not vouchsafed to us.
His age is just eleven plus
    And ever shall be so.

Tree-Nesting Cats   by Mavis Watterson

Two tall beech trees grew near our house, and our three cats, Darky, Pansy and Sparky the tom, were always climbing them after the crows' nests in the top branches. One day Darky and Pansy came to the door crying for their food, and we knew they must both have recently littered; but there was no sign of the kittens. After searching all corners of the garden in vain, we thought of the trees and watched from an upstairs window. Darky climbed one tree and Pansy the other, while Sparky sat below; but the nests were too high for us to see into them or to reach them by ladder. As the kittens grew, we could hear them crying. Some time later I again heard a yowling at the back door, and there was Pansy with a kitten in her mouth, and Sparky behind her

38

with another. Pansy brought down three more kittens, and Darky fetched hers from the other tree; all were extremely wild. Soon after this my little niece came to stay and would not leave the kittens alone. The mother cats were not having this interference and both took their kittens up the trees again until the child went home.

From Time to Time by Norman G. Suffield

I have to journey to Rochester and park my car in the cathedral precinct. I first saw Pookey, a large fluffy cat, asleep on a car bonnet. I noticed that, during the short time I was there on business, he sometimes changed cars. The weather turned colder, and one day as I drove in I saw Pookey in the distance, but had barely halted when he was alongside and, as soon as the engine stopped, he was on the bonnet. I wondered how long he took to realise that the last car in was the warmest.

CATTLE

Three against Abdul by V. O. Lonsdale

Abdul is a pedigree Jersey bull. His real name is Dairyaim Design and he is six years old. My wife, Harry the cowman, and I walked to the paddock near the farm buildings to change his head-chain. The old chain was worn and I was afraid he might snap it; he could eaily give it a direct pull when tethered in the open.

As we came up to him, Abdul put on his usual act of loud snorting and thunderous pawing of the ground. I clipped the pull-pole to his nose-ring, and Harry whipped off his old head-chain and attached the tether-chain to the ring. This was our first mistake. Abdul was now held by the pole and the tether-chain, but both were on his nose-ring. I hoped it would not break.

My wife and Harry got behind me and, kneeling on the grass, began to wrap sacking round the new chain to avoid chafing his head. That was our second mistake. We should have done this beforehand.

After a minute or two Abdul got bored and began to walk backwards – a very awkward movement to control or to stop. I pulled on the pole, but he went on backing until the tether-chain was taut. He then seemed to sit on his haunches. The nose-ring snapped and fell out of his nose. For thirty seconds we stood and looked at each other. Abdul was bewildered; I was petrified. I was thinking how awfully naked a bull looks without his usual trappings. I said, quite quietly I hope: 'Look out, the ring has broken. Get through the gate and shut it'. I could not see my wife or Harry, as I was staring steadfastly at Abdul. I don't think they wasted any time, for the gate was only twenty yards away. My wife said she would dash down to the village and get another ring. I told Harry to fetch a feed-tin with some cake and mangels from the farm. They were both away about forty minutes.

Abdul and I stood facing each other at a distance of five yards and the world seemed a very lonely place. Every time he turned his head I called sharply: 'Stand still, Abdul, you old fool'. He would instantly face me again, give me a long, baleful stare and then snort horribly. He began to dig, sending the divots flying. This was a favourite trick of his. When he has dug a hole he will grind his horns into the earth and almost stand on his head. It is a fearsome sight, if you have imagination.

After ten minutes of digging he stopped, bellowed and walked two paces towards me. I said very loudly: 'Stand still, you idiot'. He gave me another long, contemplative stare and took a lick or two of grass. He then blew in my face and I particularly noticed the strong smell of fresh grass. I spoke to him again and discussed his ancestry in detail while we continued to stare at each other with all our might.

The idea was to keep him from wandering away. The field was not fenced well enough to hold a pony and there were several gaps leading into the lane. If he walked through and turned left he had all the downs before him. If he turned right he would find himself in the village. Neither move would bear thinking about. I had to keep him near me and keep him from working out the situation. He seemed still to be wondering whether or not he was free.

At last Harry rejoined me. He rolled a mangel towards Abdul who was not interested. He then rattled the feed-tin and Abdul walked up to it and put his nose down. After a sniff he turned away; even cake held no attraction in this novel situation. Harry had brought a head-line and tried to throw it over Abdul's horns. Abdul at once leapt back, turned round and trotted away. This was our third mistake. He now knew that he could go where he liked.

At that moment my wife entered the top end of the paddock. Abdul stopped and watched her attentively till she joined us. She proudly produced two shining copper nose-rings and said: 'I think Avril is bulling. I'll go and bring her here'.

We were still being half-witted. We could not possibly have held Abdul, even if we had succeeded in getting a rope round his horns. He trotted back as soon as Avril appeared. We had retrieved one mistake, for the moment at any rate; we had drawn him away from the fence bordering the lane. Avril was not bulling after all, but Abdul hung around while we asked each other what on earth we could do. Harry said our only hope was to get him into his stall and then slip a chain over his head. I said: 'Right! Get the cows in here and we will drive the lot into the yard'.

Abdul and I once more glowered at each other until the cows arrived. Cows always know when something is up. They came galloping in with tails well up and swarmed round Abdul. We had at least shown a glimmering of sense. On the way to the yard Abdul suddenly left his wives and made for the far end of the home pasture. Harry headed him off, the sight of the rope turning him back.

In the yard with the gates firmly shut, we had our first carefree breath in two hours. Children, dogs, unsuspecting men and women were now safe, so we went in to lunch.

My wife said she would ring up the vet. He would know how to catch a bull. Other bulls must have got loose. Abdul was not the

41

only one. The vet asked if Abdul was playing the fool. We said no; he was still tickled to death at being free and was not being ferocious at all. The vet said he would be with us as soon as he could. During lunch Abdul looked into the dining-room through a window facing the yard. He gave three bellows and seemed anxious to join us.

The vet arrived with two stout ropes, each with a noose. He placed a noose on a long pea-stick, stalked the bull among the cows and neatly dropped the noose over his horns. Abdul at once galloped across the yard, but his time was up. He stopped in a corner near a telephone pole. We quietly picked up the loose end of the rope, passed it round the pole and gently drew him to it. The vet walked slowly to his head, dropped the other noose over his horns, took a turn round his nose, and secured this rope, too, to the pole. It was only a matter of minutes then to fix up Abdul with his new head-chain and two new nose-rings. We led him out to his tether again where he immediately began to eat a late lunch. I sincerely hope he thinks the whole episode was an impossible dream.

SOMERSET farmer convalescing in hospital ward: 'Zum do squeak an' zum do snort; there's gruntin' an' groanin', moanin' an' whistlin'. Zounds just like my cow yard in winnertime'.

Cow Character by Margaret Keech and Elaine R. Bullard

When I was working on a farm in the Scilly Isles, I looked after five milking cows. Two were young and characterless. The third was greedy – a scavenger that would nose round the others' mangers when they had gone and eat up their leavings; she would eat anything, that cow, though the others were fussy. Rosie was big and bossy, but I admired her will-power and influence with the rest. Jennie, the Jersey, was my favourite: she was sweet and timid.

Rosie led the herd from the fields to the milking shed and showed them to their stalls. After milking she would take them

'I would watch for the gleam in Rosie's eye'

sedately back to the field. But sometimes she took it into her head to dash over the downs for a drink at the pool, the rest following her helter-skelter, of course. So I would watch for the gleam in Rosie's eye and try to stop the charge. They had had all night in which to drink.

Then there was a narrow lane. If Rosie, in front, stopped and munched on the grassy bank, the others stopped too. When I squeezed past them to drive Rosie on, they would not follow with me in front instead of behind. Even Jennie annoyed me at such times, for she was so reserved and ladylike that a decent space had to be left between her and the rest. Evidently she disliked the proximity of her fellow-creatures, for she was always alone in one corner of the field, while the others were together in another.

M.K.

Cows are more individualistic than many folk imagine. It is well known that some are terrified of mice. My father, however, saw a commoner's cow trying to swallow a toad. Years ago I knew a Kerry-Dexter which had a craving for human hair; she would stalk any unwary picnicker with all the cunning of a scalp-hunting Red Indian. At that time I was fifteen and could have been milking in a cowshed where the ten Kerries were all older than myself, the senior matron being nineteen years old.

Cows do shed tears when in pain or distress. Two Red Polls had been brought up together from calf-hood, and even the arrival of their offspring failed to separate them. One, however, reacted to the tuberculin test and was sent away. For several weeks the other was quite obviously heart-broken and would call at the cowshed door for her friend, tears streaming down her face.

One of my most embarrassing experiences was to be 'adopted' by

'. . . trying to swallow a toad'

'She would stalk any unwary picnicker'

a Guernsey heifer. Her calf was still-born, and it appeared that her affection was transferred to me, her first attendant. Whenever possible she would follow me about, and she would leave the rest of the herd at the sound of my voice. One day her attempts to protect me from the cattle dogs thoroughly upset the herd, and a rather unpleasant stampede resulted.

'Round and round the stacks'

The most infuriating creature on four legs is a cow in a stack-yard. She will rush round and round the stacks with teats and tail flying, pausing only to toss wisps of hay into the air. Only in her own time will she suddenly sober down and stalk off quietly to her rightful place in the cowshed, as though nothing had happened. *E.R.B.*

Drawings by Marion Rivers-Moore

DEER

Autumn at Eastnor   by Elizabeth Sedgley

Lying almost hidden in the folded hills at the western end of the Malvern range, the deer park at Eastnor resounded on a fine October morning to the continuous deep bellowing of red stags in rut. Louder and more profound than the lowing of a cow with its somewhat contralto note, the vibrating roar contained something dignified, even sinister, that commanded respect. We sat in the shelter of a tree and watched a dozen stags, nearly a hundred hinds – one or two with offspring – and perhaps a score of young males with small show of antlers but seriously intending to acquire wives. Amid much complicated and restless activity, the pattern of behaviour took some time to discover. Each stag seemed concerned to hold together his hinds, who appeared superficially to be interested only in feeding. As they strayed in search of grazing, their lord became increasingly agitated and, when he sighted another stag, uttered such a series of bellows that the intruder usually halted or turned and went about. If he stopped in his tracks, the first stag was provoked to further trumpetings and deep rumblings, sometimes ending in a barking chuckle before he charged, mouth open, at the newcomer, who wisely decided that his moment was not yet. The hinds, aware of events, drifted this way and that, as if responding to a fickle breeze. At a distance one royal stag withdrew from the herd and, after pawing the ground two or three times, lowered himself for a peaceful morning's rest, dissociated from the anxieties of the rutting beasts. We left our hide-out and, keeping to the road, walked slowly into sight of one of these family groups about two hundred yards away. On our approach the hinds, encouraged by their stag, moved off towards another group; and he took up his stance, interested now in us. As we moved across his horizon, he stood on guard, watchful and still. In a few hundred yards the road turned and we lost sight of him but when, farther on, it doubled back we were astonished to find him still facing us. Not having lost our wind, he had turned through a right angle. As we watched him through field-glasses, a jackdaw took advantage of this immobile hatstand to rest on his antlers, while two others explored the worn patches on his back. Our path took us away from the valley of the deer and, as we merged into the undergrowth, the stag turned to recover his hinds. Some signal must have been passed, perhaps by their pale rump patches, for they proceeded in single file to rejoin him.

Challenge to Youth   by S. V. Tucker

Towards the end of one October I was out walking on the Quantocks when I heard a stag belling. There below me, in a coomb about five hundred yards off, was a fine old beast with seven hinds. He was roaring at three younger stags which were standing a short distance away and seemed very interested in his harem. Presently the largest of the young ones took up the challenge and started to roar too. Both pawed the ground and threw soil and bracken high into the air, back over their bodies. All the time they were getting nearer to each other, until presently they charged. They met with a crash and, with antlers locked, pushed each other round. First one had the advantage, then the other, but the old stag managed to manoeuvre so that he was higher on the slope and the young one had to give way to his superior weight. As he did so, the old stag charged and caught him in the side. That was the finish, for the young one had had enough and fled as fast as he was able, pursued for a short while by the victor. The old stag soon returned and started to offer a challenge to the others, but they evidently had no intention of taking it up; they moved off in quick time, looking back over their shoulders at the old champion which was still bellowing and pawing the ground. Meanwhile the hinds had scattered and were picking about among the furze and bracken, apparently not at all interested in the commotion. Suddenly the old stag gave himself a shake and started to get them together again. By means of many pokes and prods with his antlers, he drove them into line and then down to the wood at the bottom of the coomb, where they were lost to sight. I was lucky to see such a battle in the day-time, as these fights usually take place at night.

Sika deer by Robert Gillmor

The First Day   by Phoebe Hesketh

The spotted fawn
Awoke in small leaf-spotted suns
That quivered on his tawny back
Tattooing him with coins where he lay
Beside his mother's warmth the first long day
That gave him light:

48

The day that played him tunes
In water-music twinkling over stones
And leaf-edged undertones:
The day he learned the feel
Of dew on grass
Cool, cool and wet;
Of sun that steals the dew with sudden heat,
And heard the fret
In wind-turned willow-leaves and wrinkled pool:
The day that filled his breath with pollened wind
And smell of bracken earth and dell-deep moss:
The day he came to know
Sharp hunger and the flow
Of milk to comfort his small emptiness,
The strangeness of his legs,
The bulwark of his mother's side,
The solace of her pink tongue's first caress,
Her snow-soft belly for his sheltering,
The rhythm of untaught desires
For movement and for rest,
For food and warmth and nest
Of flattened grass to fold himself in sleep.

Sika and Roe   compiled by B.C.

When I asked what had happened to the sika deer of south
Argyll I was delighted that this brought a reply from Naomi
Mitchison of Carradale, whose 'other home' is in Botswana and
whose last letter came from Delhi, written with two hoopoes on
the lawn outside. The sika of Kintyre have moved 'slightly higher
up into the lower hills on the top edge of the forestry plantations'.
Their place has been taken by 'a plague of roe . . . They are lovely,
but when they insist that the one thing they like are my rose
bushes, varied emotions come into play. Last winter a family
climbed over the stone wall of my garden, not difficult because it
has a mass of creepers, including thick ivy stems; then they ate a

whole row of young cabbage plants, just set out'. A buck, being shooed away from her best plants by a friend, 'turned and charged her, though not perhaps as seriously as he might have done'.

I asked Richard Prior whether there was any evidence of competition between sika and roe, and he told me that in Dorset the two have distinct habitat preferences. Sika like the margins of woods and avoid the thicket stage where roe would be at home. It seems likely, therefore, that at Carradale the sika have moved out of the lower and older plantations of their own accord and the roe have moved in, just as groups of bird species replace each other at different phases of woodland development.

Service Nearly Interrupted   by Gladys Ross

We had been hearing strange vibrations on the telegraph wire attached to the house; at first we thought the wind was causing them, but they occurred also on calm and misty nights. Then we found a telegraph pole surrounded by hoof-marks, with the vegetation worn away for about 2 ft. all round the base. Stags were using it to fray off the velvet from their antlers. Eventually the pole became shaped like an hour-glass and the Post Office engineers replaced it, before it could snap in two in a gale.

DOGS

Successor   by Margaret Rhodes

This infant dog, folded in honeyed fur,
Folded in sleep, paws bunched across her nose,
Artlessly sprawls before the winter fire
And nuzzles close to us who are her world.
Twitching in dreams she lives again the chase,
Her tawny body hurled
Hilariously across the wind-wracked shore;
In dreams scuds after gulls through spume and foam
Of teasing tides; perhaps again she hears
The thin lost cries of sandpipers in her ears.

Roe fawn

Fox emerging from copse

In sleep she stretches, yawns, begins to stir;
Then stares with topaz eyes as if she saw
The dog who lay last winter in her place.
She stares and inches close
And offers us a guileless trusting paw,
Claiming us for her own – this dog we chose
To turn a house once more into a home.

The Opportunist   by E. E. Netherwood

Driving back after lunch I saw in the middle of the main road, on
the brow of the hill, what looked like a dog-fight. A closer approach
showed a long-haired dog wriggling violently on its back on a 3-ft.
sewer grating. A near-by textile dyehouse had evidently just
emptied a vat into the drain, and the dog was enjoying a Turkish
bath in the rising clouds of steam.

A Moment in the Life of a Dog   by Lord Dunsany

Outside a french window a dog looked into a drawing-room in
which his master and mistress were sitting, much hidden by furni-
ture and by a glare on the glass in which he could see tiresome
reflections of trees and a grass lawn and some daisies – all things
in which he was totally uninterested, and more than uninterested,
for they irked him intensely when his only wish, his only yearning
and longing, was to be in that drawing-room. Its romance and
mystery touched his heart more piercingly than any scene we
know can touch ours. And it was not only his sight that assured
him of this through the glare that dimmed the window, but a sort
of inner sense that he had, that all was even more wonderful than
it seemed. All he saw or guessed was corroborated by scents that
slipped under the edge of the window. Sometimes the sound of a
voice came to him, too, the voice that he always obeyed. And
between him and this seat of romance and wonder, the pane of
glass that it was sacrilege to break. If only he could be there!

Very urgently he touched the glass with the tip of a paw; but
no notice was taken. The romance of the room became more

beautiful as he waited, the boding of wonderful events to come appeared more and more dramatic. He uttered a little whine. But shut as the gates of Paradise against Adam and Eve after the Fall, the french window remained. He whined again and more mournfully than before, so mournfully that no heart could be quite so hard as to ignore that piteous appeal; and, if any heart were, the affections of that dog must have softened a little the hearts of those that owned him. There came a response to the piteous cry, and he heard through the glass every syllable. One word of it he knew well, but the tone of each syllable gave him the meaning as clearly as the one word that he knew. The exact words were, 'Oh, it's that dog again.' 'Dog' he knew perfectly clearly referred to him; for the rest he knew that some slight irritation was overcome by relenting as soon as it was uttered, and whatever the words may convey to the reader, the dog knew with the utmost clarity that the window was going to be opened. That knowledge or prophecy, whatever it be, gave a moment of bliss beyond anything that my pen can ever describe. Then the window was opened and a voice, all charm and wonder to him, said, 'Well, come in, and be quiet.' And the rapture exceeded even the joy of anticipation.

He gave a sigh of content and went to lie down on a rug that he always used, and turned round as it was his custom to do before lying down. As he turned he caught a glimpse of the lawn in the sunlight, and the hills and the sky and the wide world beyond the window, which was now shut. The scene struck him with all its beauty, as though for the first time. If only he could be there, he thought; out there where there might be rabbits and tracks in the grass and strange scents to follow. A little way off he could see the darkness of woods full of unknown beasts to be hunted, if only the window would open and he could go and see what they were and where they lurked and which of them threatened the house that he must defend. He felt that out there in the sunlight there was awaiting him a social life in which might be wonderful friendships. It was bitter to see the window shut between him and so much.

His intense yearning for all the mysteries that the wide world held in the sunlight took him back to the window, against which he lifted a pathetic paw that could not possibly open it. Once more a heart was touched by his mournful air, and again the window was opened. With one leap he was out, and there descended on him a sudden flood of happiness that is again beyond aught that my pen is able to reach. But just then there came to him the memory that only that morning he had had a flea in his head. He wondered if it might be there still. So he meditatively scratched with a hind leg several parts of his head, exploring all likely spots. And eclipsed by that activity and that wonder, all other emotions faded completely away.

Bolted Whole   by W. Rendle

During a walk from Selkirk to Bowhill on a fine May afternoon I sat down to eat my lunch by the river, where I was accosted by a black mongrel dog. He evidently expected me to share the meal, but as I had little enough for myself I shooed him away. He moved off three or four yards and began digging in the sandy soil. After only a minute he dragged out a baby rabbit about the size and shape of a large grapefruit and, to my astonishment, swallowed it whole and alive, neither biting nor chewing; then a little more digging and another baby rabbit went head first down his gullet. Apparently still hungry, he went into the shallow river, wading slowly and cautiously, peering intently into the water, though I did not see him catch any fish. In size the dog was not much bigger than a corgi, but with longer legs and very muscular shoulders and neck.

Foster-Kitten   by Marguerite Bond

I have an Alsatian bitch who is an exceptionally good mother but the avowed enemy of cats. When she first saw the kitten I had brought home, she nudged it with her nose and became quite puzzled as it wobbled towards her, fearlessly emitting endearing mews despite her warning growls. If I could arouse her maternal instinct, I thought, she might take to the kitten. So I told her to lie down, at the same time putting the kitten to her nipples and saying, 'A puppy, a sweet little puppy'. I went on repeating the word puppy. She began to lick and clean the kitten with her rough tongue, becoming so enthusiastic that she bowled it over several times; it did not seem to mind. Since then they have been inseparable, sleeping and riding in the car together. The kitten even comes for walks with us, jumping up and down the garden walls as we make our evening circuit of the block.

Keen on Sheep   by Alexander Mackenzie

When my collie Wallace vanished without trace, the sheep on the high hill at the back of my croft soon got to know that I was without a dog. They came down corries and sidewalks in hordes, like marauding tribes, to spread over my green regenerated pasture. At first I had only to call 'Wallace' at the top of my voice, and they would scuttle away to their own ground; but before long they ignored my cries. I appealed to a friend in the village, and he gave me a young dog, Afton by name.

Afton was apparently meant to be all white, but was provided, as if by an afterthought, with a glossy black coat from the top of his shoulder, down his flanks and to the rump, taking in about a quarter of his bushy tail. At the top of his head a small black cap perched precariously, like a schoolboy's on the shaggy white head of an old man. Though friendly by nature, Afton was unfortunately not keen on sheep. He regarded them with indifference, and seemed surprised when they jumped out of his way.

I put a string on him and took him after me round the sheep. He came without protest and without enthusiasm. He was loyal and obedient, but regarded any kind of restraint as punishment for some misdeed, putting on a perplexed look as if trying to recall what he had done wrong.

We collected a dozen sheep into the corner of two intersecting dykes. About six yards out, in a direct line with the corner, there was a stone pillar; and I got Afton to stand on one side of it, while I stood on the other, securely penning the animals in. I wanted him to get intimate with them: to let him see them at close quarters and get their smell into his nose. He tried to back away, but I held the string tight. It was early in the morning; there was no hurry. After a while some of the bolder sheep took a pace nearer to him, as if moved by curiosity. He shrank away with a mixed expression of fear and dislike. When I thought he had had enough for one morning, I took off the string and allowed the sheep to run with the rest. Then we rounded them all up and laboriously chased them back to their own ground. All the time Afton kept close to my heel, running when I ran and stopping when I stopped.

We repeated this performance every morning. At first the sheep took some notice of Afton's presence and behaved less stubbornly; but the days passed and he showed no inclination to learn or take an interest, just running along rather queerly at my heels. The sheep developed avoiding tactics of their own, running backwards in semi-circles or scattering in all directions.

A routine of such high tension could not last; a climax was inevitable. It came after ten days. One sunny morning we got the sheep back as far as the moor, where the heather grows like brushwood. They were strung out in a line, and at each end they persistently edged back, lengthening the line all the time. It took me a quarter of an hour to walk from one end to the other. I had chased some back from behind boulders at the far end of the left wing when I saw a batch at the outside of the right wing moving at speed back to the green grazing. I ran, and Afton ran after me, keeping close to my heels as usual. There were ditches to jump and soft bogs from which I had to pull my feet with effort. Half way across I was breathing hard, my heart was thumping and there was a knocking in my head. Then the toe of my boot caught in some stringy heather, and I fell on my face.

When I struggled to my feet in a daze, I felt that some time must have passed. There was no sheep, and Afton was not about. I took a few paces forward to the brink of an incline, and there in the hollow were all the sheep packed close, like a ball, with Afton running round and round them. Then, as if he had noticed me looking, he dived into their midst, scattered them and, with a swift race round, gathered them together again. They were terrified and packed together as close as they could get.

After a while I called him off. He came immediately, panting hard, tongue hanging out, jaws wide part, seeming as if his head would split open. He sat on his tail as close to my leg as he could get, and I could feel the pounding of his heart. There was a comradeship in his hugging that he had not shown before. 'Now,' he seemed to be saying, 'both of us are keen on sheep'.

A Dog's Memory   by Margaret Malcomson

Banshee of Versida was the youngest of four pedigree Alsatians which went with their owners some years ago to settle in East Africa. On arrival by rail at Nairobi, while the dogs were waiting for the vets, Banshee escaped, tore out of the station and made for the open country. For two days game scouts, police and Africans searched and failed to recover her, though they found her spoor in the soft mud of the Athi river. Then, sadly, her owners continued their journey to their new home in the Kenya highlands.

Two and a half years later a young farmer, on his way to deliver milk in Nairobi, was told by his African assistant that a European dog was running with wild dogs on the plains. Returning home he spoke to his father, who advised him to take out the closed car and, if he saw the dog, to race it until it tired. This he did, and the dog, being in a deplorable condition, became exhausted and sank to the ground. The farmer crept towards the animal, coaxing and wooing it, and presently got it in front of him in the direction of the car. When he was quite close he clapped his hands and said 'up', and the dog jumped in. Then the trouble began, for the dog took charge, walking from side to side of the car, snarling and baring its teeth. It was an hour and a quarter before the farmer was able to enter.

He drove home, got the dog into a horse-box and informed the police, who telegraphed to the people who had lost Banshee. They hurried to the farm, but when they looked inside the horse-box they were quite certain that this bag of bones with brindled head, pitted sides and torn underlip could not be the missing dog. The farmer pointed out that the head was not brindled but a mass of dried blood and scars; and after some discussion the visitors decided to take a chance on it. On the journey home the wife kept an eye on the dog, and presently she asked her husband to go on talking as it was listening, with its head first on one side and then on the other. Suddenly the dog put its paws on the back of the driver's seat and licked his hair, ears and collar. He stopped the car, and what Banshee said to her master and what he said to her cannot be put into print.

When they arrived home a vet was summoned, but Banshee would allow no-one to go near her except her master. With much nursing and a great deal of affection she began to recover; the old obedience and police tests were tried, and after a few moments' hesitation she remembered and obeyed. For a long time, however, she would wake up with a scream and stand trembling until her master's hand reassured her.

A Dog's Life   by Jessie Hickford

However sober and controlled when working in harness, my guide dog certainly makes up for it when she is running free. On one jaunt we set out along a narrow sea wall across the East Mersea salt marshes. I held my friend's arm and slipped off the leash. Away went an excited, happy dog. I heard her rush down the slope of the sea wall. Splash! She had found a ditch. I heard her flounder about, then crash round in the reeds and grass. Next moment she was up the slope to share her pleasure with us, shaking water everywhere. I lost count of the times she zig-zagged up and down in front of us as we walked along. A rather louder splash: 'Now what has she done?' She had belly-flopped, I was told, straight into a somewhat larger dyke and was swimming along happily. She scrambled out so exhilarated that she rushed to and fro.

When she so obviously delights in fresh air, water and freedom, I marvel how patiently she will sit at a crossing in the streets of Colchester and watch the noisy, stinking vehicles, before leading me safely across the road.

Suddenly there was a surprised girl's cry and suppressed laughter from my friends. Prudence in her hunt-about, they explained, had flushed out a pair of young lovers hidden deep in the reeds. I could imagine their shocked surprise when a large wet dog appeared nosing through the reeds. Back at the car, we wrapped a rug round a dear dirty dog and bundled her into the back seat, and there she slept for the whole journey home.

A Dog's Disgust   by G. Tindale

Reading 'Manners makyth dog' reminded me of a grand gun dog my father had, a pointer named Juno. His farm was at Elvington, near York, which had good game shooting. In Dad's later years when his health was not too good, if he missed with the first shot the old dog would sit on her hind legs and look up to his face. If he missed with the second shot, Juno would turn round and go home and nothing could bring her back that day.

DORMICE

Return of the Dormouse?   by Kenneth Underwood

The common dormouse is undoubtedly one of Britain's most attractive mammals and the text-book will tell you that it measures about $5\frac{1}{2}$ in. (including tail), is golden brown in colour with paler

Dormouse by Robert Gillmor

undersides, has a fairly bushy tail, large liquid jet black eyes, and long whiskers. It is a charming sight sitting upright like a squirrel, eating food held in its front feet but, sad to say, it is seldom seen because not only is the dormouse nocturnal but it also hibernates from approximately October to May.

61

Dormouse, a scraperboard by Kenneth Underwood

The dormouse has long been considered rare and I had come to regard it as well nigh extinct. Having spent my childhood in the Dorset countryside, I became familiar at an early age with most of the British mammals to be found in the South West except, that is, the elusive dormouse for which countless searches through the hazel coppices proved fruitless.

During the summer of 1970 I was engaged on a series of sketches depicting British wildlife and I became obsessed with the idea of finding a dormouse to study at first hand: not that I really expected any success. The disappearance of hazel coppice and hedgerows, and the general encroachment of urban development had, I thought, diminished further any hope of finding one, and I was unable even to contact anyone who had seen a dormouse. Nevertheless I alerted every possible source likely to prove fruitful.

During the last week in August I received word from forestry workers, engaged in cleaning operations at Everleigh, Wiltshire, that they had discovered a number of empty nests in the dense undergrowth. This was excitement enough but in the first week of September a nest was recovered intact with four babies. Their eyes were just open and they looked rather like miniature lion cubs. The parents had fled in the face of devastation and the babies had to be hand fed on Horlicks for nearly two weeks, when they abruptly turned to solids. To give them the maximum chance of survival a naturalist friend took two of the litter and all four are still in good health. It is hoped to breed from them in captivity with the object of releasing the offspring when self-supporting.

But the discovery of dormice at Everleigh in September was not the end, only the beginning. I next heard of nests of youngsters found at Whitsbury in Hampshire and Bovington in Dorset. This was soon followed by the discovery of a number of empty nests at Clarendon, just south of Salisbury, while back at Everleigh the forestry workers continued to discover empty nests. At Clarendon nests occupied by adult dormice were found in mid-November and, although several cold spells had occurred in October, they were still fully active and showing no inclination to hibernate.

It is interesting to note that there is evidence of dormice in some numbers at Bovington in surroundings far removed from the popular conception of the dormouse habitat: hazel coppice with dense undergrowth. These Bovington dormice were in heathland predominantly covered by gorse and some distance from the nearest hazel. This raises the question of food which appears to be derived from the occasional oak and beech tree in the vicinity, although the dormouse has always been regarded as none too partial to the acorn. There are ample supplies of blackberries and rose hips but one wonders what the Bovington dormouse uses to fatten himself for hibernation. In the absence of the hazel nut one must assume that it is equally content with the acorn and beech nut.

Now that we have met in person, I find the dormouse smaller and less fluffy (especially the tail) than I had imagined, but very much more active. It runs and jumps with amazing speed and is an incredibly skilful climber. Our dormice quickly settled down and I have discovered to date that in captivity they will eat apples, pears, cake and lettuce. On one occasion an escapee completely demolished a cineraria during the night without any adverse after-effects.

It may well be that the dormouse was never as rare as had been assumed, but that its long hibernation and nocturnal habits have kept it out of the naturalist's eye. Alternatively, it could be that, although hazel coppice and hedgerow have rapidly decreased, so also have many of the predators of the dormouse. I would be interested to know to what extent the dormouse has been observed in recent years in other parts of the country. Is it possible that their numbers are increasing?

Studies of our dormice during the winter of 1970–71 showed that they do not truly hibernate in captivity. The cages were kept in an unheated room and it was found that during the coldest spells the dormice emerged, on average, on alternate nights to feed, but otherwise there was little activity. Except during the coldest of spells, the dormice appeared about 9 p.m., were active through the night, and returned to their sleeping at dawn. This routine was most regular. It was also observed that even during the day-time any disturbance to the cage would bring forth an inquisitive face, indicating that the dormouse was sleeping rather than hibernating.

This disinclination to hibernate may be attributable to the fact that the present captives were obtained from very late litters in the autumn of 1970 and had no opportunity to fatten themselves as do the wild dormice. They were barely weaned when most dormice are supposed to go into hibernation. One wonders whether they might have perished had they not been caught. It was found in 1970 that dormice were producing young in some numbers during late August and early September, which belonged, presumably, to second and even third litters. By the time such late litters are weaned the food supply is declining and cold weather is approaching, and it may be that considerable numbers, unprepared for the winter, perish.

The problem is whether these young dormice will breed in captivity after a somewhat unnatural start to life. With the arrival of spring and the early summer of 1971 the dormice appeared again in the locations now known, and adults have been obtained from Clarendon and Bovington and paired with the original dormice from Everleigh.

Every endeavour has been made in housing the dormice to create an environment resembling conditions in the wild as closely as possible. Large cages have been provided with a network of hazel twigs and natural props such as turves, dead leaves, moss and logs. At the time of writing it is too early to be certain of success but one pair at least have been observed mating.

FOXES

Odd Man In   by B. G. Palmer
On a winter's morning with a light snow cover a vixen called her strangled cry along a woodland ride, near a junction of paths

where the ground was covered with foxes' tracks and the air heavy with their strong scent. We left the wood and were following a hedgerow when a vixen and dog fox also emerged some 200 yds. away and began to cavort about the field. We crouched in the ditch and, as I watched through binoculars, I saw a second dog fox make his way towards the pair. The two dogs started to fight, sweeping round in circles and occasionally making rushes at each other. The vixen withdrew a short distance, sat down and watched. Through the corner of my eye I saw a movement at the edge of the wood and out stepped a third dog fox, bigger and much darker than the other two. He trotted over to the vixen, who made up to him; and both ran towards us, leaving the fight in progress. As they drew near, I noticed that the vixen was running low to the ground, obviously tired after being hounded by the dog foxes. The two leapt the ditch and disappeared into the wood only 20 yds. from us. The others then stopped fighting, nosed the wind and ran into the wood.

The Skeleton   by Jean Kenward

A few bones, flagrant in the November stillness:
What are they, fox or stoat?
Not a fragment of pelt remains, the winter's wool-thick
Mist their only coat.
I remember the fox I encountered suddenly
Seeming a little more
Solid than sunlight, apricot-coloured and splendid,
Warm on the grey hoar.
For a moment we paused in startled recognition,
Then like a king
He turned his back on the dross of my admiration,
Loped off, not hurrying,
Knowing himself the finer of the pair of us;
And I went my way.
I could wish that I had not stumbled upon this broken
Carcass, today.

Fox, a scraperboard by Kenneth Underwood

Raishy   by Lady Braid-Taylor

I was gardening when my son appeared with a small shapeless
bundle, a pale greyish fawn in colour. It had been found under a
haystack in a tunnel of twigs which contained four minute cubs –
three vixens and a fox. The vixens had been killed before my son
arrived, and the little fox was whimpering pitifully in a piece of old
newspaper in a broken coal-scuttle. Half a crown changed hands,
and Horatio, as we called him (Raishy for short), was carried home.
My helper in rearing and training him was my son's Labrador,
Brucey. He washed Raishy while I fetched my golf jacket. We put
the cub inside and I felt him snuggle contentedly into the small of
my back. He was no trouble. When the calls of nature caused dis-
comfort, Raishy kicked me and was put on the ground. Every two
hours he had a small amount of tepid milk and water from a baby's
bottle. We fed him day and night for five weeks. I always wore the
golf jacket, whatever else I had on; at night I had to sleep in it – if
you can call sitting up in bed with this strange creature sleeping.

The day after his arrival we heard a fox barking. For four or five days we noticed behind the cupressus hedge a flattened place, where some animal had been sleeping, and perhaps waiting. Three weeks later I was sitting on the lawn, and Raishy was playing with the cat on the verandah. Suddenly I saw, in a triangle with the cub and myself, the vixen. If I let her get him, he would have no home and little chance of survival, but if I tried to reach him she might, in the manner of vixens, go for me. Quietly I walked over to the cub and picked him up. The vixen looked at me uncertainly, and then slunk off across the garden.

I had to go daily into the town to the shops. While Horatio was still in my golf jacket, he had to come too. He was the model of tact on the bus and also in the cinema. On these occasions, among the empty shopping bags was one which contained milk, a bottle, and a small saucepan. I shall never forget the butcher's face when I asked him for the loan of his gas ring. I think he thought I was ill, and he took me into a cubicle adjoining the office. There Raishy lay guzzling happily, clinging to the teat with two paws, while the butcher, his sister and the entire queue looked on.

At six months old Raishy began to smell to high heaven, so he had to have a house built outside, where he does not smell at all. When he dislikes any food he throws his plate round the pen. Among other things he likes cooked rhubarb, and cooked and raw rabbit. He will sit for hours listening to dance music, but I am glad to say honky-tonk makes him restless and irritable. His language is expressive: 'ha ha ha' registers joy, 'foofh' means disgust, and 'huh' tells you that he is angry and sulky. One night he was attacked by a germ which left him blind in one eye. I called in a vet, and he said the other eye had practically gone too, and that Raishy should be destroyed However, with M and B and vitamins I had Horatio cured in one eye within a week. For months he was blind in the other eye, but he was still just as full of fun. Living outdoors has cured it, and now he has perfect sight. He gambols in his pen, knowing he can go out, and I know he will come back. One day the call of the wild may get him, but I doubt it.

(above) *Nanny and kid;* (below) *holiday friendship*

Farmyard serenade

FROGS

Enoch the Frog   by E. W. Winterbottom

One October evening I heard something splash into the water
trough in my greenhouse, and found a young frog in the weed
growing round the trough. In time I used to look for him whenever
I went into the greenhouse; I christened him Enoch and started
to feed him to find out what he lived on. He accepted woodlice,
worms, slugs, earwigs, snails and anything else that moved and
was not too big for him to tackle. His favourite dish was woodlice, if
he was given a choice. He would seize a large worm by its middle
and be thrown all over the place, but would stick to it until they
both fell into the trough, from which he would emerge again with
a satisfied look. At first I thought he deliberately drowned the
worm, but I came to the conclusion that it was only by accident.
The evening visit to Enoch became a ritual with all my young
friends. We searched under stones for slugs or worms, went into
the greenhouse and called 'Enoch'. He was rarely in sight when
we entered, but after several calls he was there. When we dropped
his meal on the floor, he would cock his head on one side and skip
round it, and it was gone. His tongue picked up a slug too quickly
for us really to see it. His capacity for slugs gradually went up from
two to five. If a worm was too large for his stomach he would
swallow as much as possible, sit for several minutes with about
an inch of it hanging from his mouth, and then gulp down the
remainder. His favourite sleeping place was in the hollow of a
brick about two inches below the hot-water pipes; he liked his
back warm. I thought several times that he was getting on the
benches among the plants and wondered how he did it. Then one
evening I saw him going up; he climbed the ferns by the water
trough. He kept the greenhouse free from pests. Sometimes the
door was left open, but he stayed inside. In early June I fumigated
the greenhouse and placed Enoch outside in a bucket with plenty
of cover. Later I put him back, but he did not like it and departed
the following morning.

GOATS

Snow-white Milk   by Freda Downton

When Snow came to us she was just weaned and small enough for me to carry. She was a British Saanen goat, white and hornless, gentle and affectionate. She arrived only because my husband, viewing our half-acre of wilderness, remarked, 'What we want is a goat. They eat anything.' A book informed us that 'anything' included ivy, gorse, brambles, nettles, all of which goats ate 'with relish'. The thought of our wilderness being gorged with relish was irresistible. But before Snow grew into an adult we had unexpectedly moved house and we left behind us our wilderness, little changed from the pre-Snow days. In its place she had a lush meadow but until the garden fence was made goat-proof it was a common sight to see Snow ravaging the roses. Came the dreadful day when she ate rhododendrons, poisonous to goats, and the vet only just managed to pull her through. It was he who discovered she needed milking. 'But she's never been mated!' I exclaimed. He explained that nanny goats can be maiden milkers and so every day I went to the shed with my saucepan and emerged an hour later with half a pint of beautifully white, frothy milk. Introducing the family to goat's milk was not easy. My husband did not like it in his tea and my mother took a dislike to it after drinking a glass 'neat'. Eventually I won everyone over with the delicious puddings it made. Before long we could not distinguish it from cow's milk. Encouraged, I mated our maiden milker. After kidding she gave four pints a day and I was able to do something we had never dreamed of – cancelled the milkman.

'Wild' Goats   by Henry Tegner

Little appears to be known about the origins of the wild goats which frequent mountainous districts of England, Wales and Scotland, but they were no doubt largely haphazard. An instance of the way in which a small herd may be formed came to my notice recently when I was inquiring about the Langleeford herd that used to frequent the south-eastern flanks of Cheviot. I learned that the whole herd had perished during the hard winter of 1946-47. Since then, however, the shepherd on the ground has released a tame nanny, which has quickly adapted herself to feral conditions, and he hopes soon to be able to release a male on the hill. When I asked him why he had acted in this way, he told me that he liked to see goats on his hills: they provided variety to the landscape.

There are a number of other reasons why hill folk like to have goats on the hill. In Scotland and, at one time, in the far north of England, when cattle rather than sheep ranged the hills, it was believed that a goat running among them was an insurance against contagious abortion. Whether there is any scientific evidence for this, I have failed to discover. Goats are also considered to be deadly enemies of adders, which the males are thought to attack and kill. This belief undoubtedly exists in certain parts of Northumberland, but I have not yet found a man who has seen a goat kill an adder. Finally, goats are believed to be extremely sensitive to pending snow and storms, so that they come low and seek shelter in advance of sheep, thus warning shepherds what to expect. Unfortunately the goats themselves appear to suffer in very severe weather. During my investigations I have come across more than one instance of a whole herd, or the majority of one, having succumbed in heavy snowstorms. A herd was exterminated some years ago in the Cairngorm mountains in central Scotland. I have already mentioned the fate of the Langleeford herd in the winter of 1946–47 when the Whickhope herd, which inhabited territory in the North Tyne valley, near Kielder, also succumbed. [The belief that a goat running with cattle will save them from disease is still found in various parts of Britain, but our inquiries have brought no explanation of it from scientists. – *Editors*.]

The Little White Goat   by Paul Henry

Jimmy, the gardener, was old and ineffective, but he had one virtue which helped to make up for his many deficiencies: he was devoted to animals – all animals – and gave to these stray dogs and half-starved cats all the affection which a childless old age had denied to him. Jimmy had been given a little goat as a present by a man who really wanted to get rid of it, and the gardener had taken it to his bosom.

I was living at the time in a wild, rock-strewn, treeless part of County Wicklow and a little flock of semi-wild goats had made this barren tract their home and bred there. From time to time these had been joined by others and now there was a respectable herd of some thirty to forty, which roamed the valleys among the rocks and gorse.

The little white goat was beautiful to look at in a dainty feminine way; when she broke into a run beside her master and kicked up her heels in a little pirouette, nothing could have been prettier, and she was milk-white. Her tiny feet were always well groomed; I half suspected the old man of scrubbing them. So pretty and distinguished did the little goat look in the meadow that I allowed her to be brought into the garden, where she was always securely tethered, for I knew how destructive goats can be. In a few weeks she became as one of the family; but she never wandered far from Jimmy, who took off her lead when she left the garden, and she frisked on the hillside as she followed him home, playing round him as he went.

She had never been known to have any 'followers', until one day Jimmy came with the news that he had found her wandering away some distance from her home and had, with difficulty, caught her and brought her back. The gardener, who for a country-man was very innocent, failed to notice that the little goat might often be seen looking longingly towards the mountains where the wild goats lived, and snuffling the air. She still looked as demure as ever, but several times Jimmy had found her wandering, always in the direction of the hills. One day, though no-one had noticed her leaving the garden, the little kid was seen by several people heading for the mountains and it appeared as if she was in no hurry to return.

Jimmy was old, but sturdy enough, and he started in pursuit. A young goat can be one of the most agile of animals, and the com-

74

bined efforts of a half a dozen boys failed to secure her. Jimmy was despondent at his loss and, although he saw her often enough in the distance, she refused to come within reach. She was going wild, but she was still snow-white and the little hooves looked as polished as ever.

One evening about a fortnight later, I was going through the mountains and had reached a spot which I knew to be a favourite haunt of the goats during the rutting season, when I surprised a herd of thirty or forty wild goats. Near the centre of them, separated from her fellows and dazzling white, stood the little goat. A large black buck with terrific horns shambled towards her and, as he did so, from some distance away, a brindled buck with equally big horns moved forward. The two bucks stopped and looked at each other; the rest of the herd moved slowly in their direction. The little goat, now standing alone, bent over and scratched her back delicately and with precision with one horn; her toilet was then complete.

I drew a little nearer and sat down. From my position I had a good view of the whole flock about twenty feet away; they all stopped eating and looked at me curiously and then, evidently coming to the conclusion that I meant them no harm, began eating again. The rivals halted. I could see them watching each other with their long, slanting, green eyes. They were uneasy; taking a few steps here and there aimlessly, they would throw up their heads and look long and fixedly at each other, their eyes aflame with anger and desire They were now within striking distance and reared up to their full height, then dropped to their feet again, still facing each other; their action, with feet firmly planted and arched necks, reminded me of something I had once seen on a Greek coin. This movement was repeated several times and was, I took it, part of their love ritual. But it was only a preliminary, for with a savagery that had to be seen to be believed they hurled themselves at each other; the crash of their skulls, as they met, sounded across the little valley and the whole herd stood in a circle to watch them.

No quarter was given. I noticed that every advantage was taken of the slightest rise of the ground, and was amazed at the rapidity with which they circled round and round, seeking a more favourable position and a firmer stance. This was no love play; the straining haunches and bloodshot eyes told a different story. Yet the horns, formidable things nearly two and a half feet long and shaped like a kris, were never used, although an upward thrust from one of these dangerous weapons, with lowered head, would have felled an ox The ground was torn and scarred as they twisted, slipped and turned, and their massive heads crashed together in a way that I thought no bone could resist. For one fleeting second, and for the first time, I caught a look of indecision – or was it fear? – in the eyes of the brindled buck, and he winced as the two skulls crashed together again. The look of indecision and the wince showed me plainly that the duel was nearly over; all the other goats knew it too for they started to move slowly away. He made a sudden movement as if to continue the fight, but thought better of it.

A few minutes after this savage encounter of the rivals, the vanquished buck was quietly eating the sweet grass of the hillside. The victor stood waiting while the little goat, apparently quite unconcerned, stooped to nibble a blade of grass, then changed her mind, and with a happy frisk began to practise the steps of her interrupted minuet.

A Detective Story   by F. G. Turnbull

Below the sixty- or seventy-feet-high rocky bank of the stream where I stood lay the dead bodies of four ewes. Two had their necks broken; the others were smashed up generally. The fate of the ewes surprised me. Sheep had grazed in the field for many years, and such a mishap had never before occurred. I could only suppose that the ewes had been feeding in a group close to the edge and that the ground had given way beneath their combined weight. When I climbed up and saw the farmer, he was incredulous about the dead ewes until he looked over and saw the bodies. Near the edge there were trees, and I noticed that some of their bark had been nibbled away. 'Look, Sam,' I said, 'here's what's happened. They've been standing up at the trees eating the lichen, and they've fallen off.' The farmer looked closely at the trunks. 'Tha'rt reight; they hev an' all, but –' Sam broke off when we heard a thin, tremulous bleat. There, perched on her hind legs against a tree, and with a strip of lichen dangling from her munching jaws, was a young goat. 'It's noan been the sheep that et the trees after all,' he said, 'it's been Phyllis. She were aye gettin' into mischief, so I put her wi' t' ewes last week.' Phyllis stood affectionately chewing the pocket of Sam's jacket as we considered the matter further. The only conclusion we could arrive at was that the sheep had been startled when feeding beneath the trees and had crowded each other over the edge. A few days later, I was wading up the stream in search of trout. I glanced toward the spot where the dead sheep had lain. There, to my surprise, lay another ewe. This was becoming serious. I went to look for Sam. When I told him of his further misfortune he seemed very worried indeed. We got the cart and brought the ewe to the yard. Sam had skinned the animal when he motioned to me and pointed out some peculiar abrasions on the flesh – red blotches about the size of a halfpenny. They were in pairs, about four inches apart. 'That looks odd, Sam,' I said. 'T' others were a' t' same,' he replied. I wondered if there might be a projection on the steep bank face that the sheep could have struck in its descent. I returned to the scene of the disaster trying to fathom the mystery. I viewed the place from above and below, but could find no solution to the problem. Still, I was positive that those red blotches were in some way connected with the death of the animals. I decided to return in the early hours of the following morning and keep watch from the opposite bank. Dawn was just breaking when I approached the bank top. While still a little distance away, I heard the 'baa-aa' of a sheep in distress, so I ran. On reaching the bank-top I lay down in the grass and focused my glasses. There, near the edge, I could see a ewe and – Phyllis. The sheep was panting as though from exertion and seemed in fear of the goat. Presently the ewe made a frantic dash for the field behind her. Phyllis immediately charged at her, driving her down the bank again. The sheep once more essayed to pass upward, and Phyllis leapt forward to intercept her. The ewe dodged but was no match for the nimble goat. A vicious dig of the goat's horns sent her stumbling down again. Then Phyllis resumed her grazing. A few moments later the ewe tried once more to pass by the very edge. The goat wheeled swiftly and charged, a four-legged battering ram, at the sheep, and knocked her clean over the edge.

Bringing up Mayflower   by June Severn

May 4. 9.30 a.m. Beauty shows signs of approaching labour. Stand by all morning to remove and destroy kids before she has time to lick them. 1 p.m. Beauty cudding happily. 4.30 p.m. Worn out with innumerable fruitless excursions down garden, retire to kitchen to brew tea. 5 p.m. Discover fine vigorous nanny kid – only one, thank goodness – washed and fed and up on its long wobbly legs. Go completely jelly-hearted; Mayflower is reprieved.

May 5. Beauty has scratched away clean straw and put kid to sleep on damp bricks. Mayflower very cold. Let both out in their run. Mayflower does little experimental dance in the buttercups. All very charming, but feel abysmally ignorant about proper way to start her on road to become useful milking goat. 2 p.m. Long talks on telephone with more experienced goat-keepers. Won over to the idea that bottle feeding is best in long run. Borrow baby's bottle, and rush out to buy lambing teat. 3 p.m. Beauty paws child about very roughly, and evidently believes that cleanliness is next to godliness. Pen Mayflower in grassy alley between goat paddock and hedge. Beauty quite content to watch Mayflower, who appears delighted to escape from incessant washing. 6 p.m. Lure Beauty into her house with tit-bits, and bring kid indoors; little fuss from either. Mayflower can't keep her balance on slippery kitchen lino. Put her in outsize tuck box. Sadie, a virgin bitch of seven, over-come with maternal feelings, gets in box too, but is disappointed to find Mayflower rather knobbly. Cat looks pained and leaves house with dignity. Slight tussle over first bottle, rather less at 10 p.m. Two teeth in front, and blue eyes like a kitten.

May 6–8. Mayflower grows almost while we look at her. Very lively in the kitchen. Practises jumping on and off chairs until she can do it neatly. Apparently naturally house-trained. Plays every evening in garden with dog, who is rather overpowered by her somersaults and curveting – a most eccentric 'puppy'!

May 9. For first time Mayflower recognises bottle from afar and comes running for it. Take 12 to 15 oz. at each of four feeds, sucking so hard that she gets a frothy moustache. Removes this gracefully with a hind hoof, unless she can wipe her mouth on somebody's clothes. In afternoon to a neighbouring breeder to have horn buds removed – not a job for an amateur. Troubles soon forgotten in a bottle. Like her mother, Mayflower is easily comforted with food.

May 10–13. Mayflower growing like mad, and beginning to fill out. Tries to pull down leaves like the grown-ups, sucks them, and spits them out. Spends most of day doing stunts on top of her shelter. Tyrannises over Beauty by perpetually calling her down to the fence, and then running away. Up at home, dustbin and coal bucket have a fatal fascination.

May 14. First walk on collar and lead with the dog. Both very excited. Mayflower proceeds in series of bounds, but does not drag like a puppy. Extremely intelligent, but quite unlike dog or cat. The human voice does not seem to register, although she recognises us from a distance and is very affectionate. Terrific powers of observation. Watches Beauty intently and usually repeats an action correctly the first time.

May 15. Now eight teeth in front, and any number, top and bottom, at back. Eyes turning yellow.

May 16. Jumps out of run into vegetable garden. Shows no inclination to suck mother, so turned into goat paddock. Speedily has Beauty properly under her hoof. Snow White, the scrub, horns her gently but firmly when she becomes too rampageous. Decide to keep her indoors at night a little longer.

May 17. Mayflower can now jump out of her box. No longer ideal household pet. Has about doubled her size and weight. Rises three feet vertically in air and descends on kitchen table. Leaps on the cat, who is slumbering uneasily on dresser. (Mayflower has annexed his chair.) Forages for sticky paper in rubbish box. Sadie sadly disillusioned that her 'puppy' has grown up so fast.

May 18. Mayflower now manages grass quite well, but finds hay a bit tough. Has discovered delights of burnt-out bonfire and hen run. Tap-dances on roof of duck house. Scales roof of hen house and can't get down. In two weeks our furry blue-eyed baby has become a grubby little hoyden, but it is still the most engaging baby animal I have ever met.

HARES

Problem in a Sand-Pit   **compiled by B.C.**

By the estuary of the river Bann in Northern Ireland Peg Pollock found a cottage that is a naturalist's 'natural'. The addition of a large plate-glass window has made one room into a comfortable hide. In a single sweep of the telescope – kept at the ready night and day – I have counted ten species of wader, with gulls and ducks, feeding on the falling tide; but birds are not the only attraction. After the foot-and-mouth scare early in 1968 and the ban on shooting, Irish hares increased locally and became, as Peg Pollock wrote, 'beautiful and frequent visitors' to her field of view, where they developed a taste for autumn hawkbit, 'biting off the stalk at the base, then nibbling up to and eating the flower. In June I watched one scrape and eat sand in a small pit near by; for about half an hour it hopped from place to place, choosing particular dark strata, to scratch them deeply and bite out mouthfuls. At Treetops I have watched elephants dig up with their tusks clods of the salt- and mineral-soaked soil, place them on their looped trunks and so feed them into their mouths. So I believe my hare was searching the richest veins in the sand to satisfy its needs.'

She took two colour slides which clearly show the scratch-marks in the sand.

I referred this observation to Winwood Reade, who has been studying hares at close quarters for several years. It reminded her of behaviour she had seen only once, early on a May morning in 1965. 'Two does and a buck had been following their usual pattern of resting, grooming and feeding about six to eight lengths apart. Just before six o'clock the doe which was leading the way suddenly started to move about much faster in a small area, alternately humping her body high and putting her head down to scratch at bare patches of soil between the grass. I watched her carefully through binoculars and came to the conclusion that, although her chin rested on the ground in a darting movement, she was not feeding but sniffing the soil. My notes read: "She is more like a buck on a scent trail than typical feeding". There is no doubt that scent is of great significance in the life of a hare. "Chinning" is the deposition of a secretion from the gland in the skin of the lower jaw on various objects, usually after exploratory sniffing.' Winwood Reade added that sand from the pit should be tested for its salt content.

It was not until quite recently that I had a chance to take a sample. By then the original face had fallen away, but I collected sand from the darkest strata I could find, and this contains one per cent salt by weight. Supposing that salt enters the sand when the wind blows up the estuary, the amount in the surface layers could vary; and there may have been a higher content when Peg Pollock watched her hare, as she is quite positive, biting the sand.

Hares on the Hill   by Alex Tewnion

Mountain hares are thin on the ground in my favourite region for wild-life photography, the Cairngorms. But a friend told me that they were plentiful on hills near Crieff in central Scotland. After an exploratory visit I chose for their study an area of about 600 acres rising from the valley floor and Loch Turret, at about 1175 ft., to the top of a long ridge which sloped gently northward to the summit of Choinneachain Hill (*c.* 2550 ft.). A large corrie, much of it visible from a point on the ridge, formed about one-third of the area. Ridge, hill and corrie are mostly covered with heather and some grass, and the ground is grazed by sheep; it also carries a large population of grouse.

The choice was a good one, for the density of mountain hares there proved to be as great as anywhere in Scotland. The ground was largely snow-covered on the winter day of my initial survey; but long narrow strips of vegetation were exposed, and the hares were loosely grouped on them. I often had ten or twelve or more in view at one time with the unaided eye. The largest number I saw together was sixty-three, on a stretch of heather and grass measuring 300 yds. by 40 yds. in the corrie; and I have since seen similar concentrations elsewhere. An accurate estimate is difficult to make, but at the end of March 1969, when I took a four-mile walk up the hillside, along the ridge and down the corrie, a careful count totalled 157; and I was reasonably sure that few had been included twice. This gave a figure of one to four acres and, as I viewed only half the ground, the true density was probably at least double this.

From November to mid April the hares are in their white winter coats and easy to spot on snow-free ground; even those hidden in long heather often betray themselves by watchful white heads peeping above the vegetation. From about the middle of March onwards, when they are moulting to the 'blue' summer coat, great variation is apparent between individuals. Hares on the higher ground are said to remain white longer than those lower down, but I often saw whiter ones below 1500 ft. in Glen Turret in April than at over 2500 ft. on the Cairnwell in the Grampians.

In winter and early spring, when the snow cover is 50 per cent or more, I found the hares to be fairly tame. Even walking quite openly, I could approach to within 100 yds. of many before they became alert, and to 50 yds. before they ran away. When a hare alerts, it first pricks its ears, then sits erect on its hind-legs with forefeet on the ground. In a hollow it will stand upright with its forefeet clear of the ground to get a better view, and occasionally it does this also in the open. When in the hollow, it raises its head slowly until its eyes are just clear of the obstruction, and pulls its ears flat so that its head maintains a smooth contour. The sight of another hare or of sheep running, or the alarm call of red grouse, curlew, golden plover and other birds, will alert a hare and often send it tearing away without waiting to discover the cause. When danger threatens, some run off slowly for 40 or 50 yds. before stopping to sit up on their hind-legs and watch. Then they run a similar distance, stop for another survey and, after half a minute, are off again – a sequence that may be repeated many times. Others in seemingly identical circumstances will run 400 yds. or more at full stretch before they stop. It is not true that they always run uphill when frightened, as is often claimed.

After some practice I was able to overcome the habitual caution of some hares by moving very slowly and carefully towards them when they were either dozing or feeding. A normally alert individual, if the observer remains quite still, will gradually relax and eventually resume its previous activity – resting, sunning, dozing or feeding. Mountain hares often dig into peat banks, and many on the Choinneachain Hill had burrows from 1 to 3 ft. in length and even longer; and they would rest and doze at the entrances during the warmer daylight hours.

I always carry a pair of 10 × 50 binoculars in the field. With them I can tell easily at 100 yds. if a hare is sleeping, dozing or merely sunning itself. I found it impossible to approach a resting animal; but mountain hares doze with their eyes only half open, and then only sudden movements seem to register sufficiently on their retinas to trigger off a reaction, for I was able to stalk a number during these spells. The stalking was an exacting and sometimes painful pursuit, for the hare dozes fitfully. Every few seconds, or at intervals of up to a minute at times, it opens its eyes fully and its nostrils wide, wrinkling its nose as if to test the air for scents. The slightest movement will then send it scurrying away, so the stalker-photographer may have to freeze with one foot in mid air and a 7-lb. camera held in a most awkward position. It took me almost an hour to cover 80 yds. through deep snow to get a series of pictures. I had taken so long to approach to within 20 ft. that I believe it had come to accept me as part of the landscape. I was on its leeward side, so it could not catch the tell-tale human scent.

Hares doze in the open sunshine with legs tucked under them; but in deep sleep they lie on one side with all four legs stretched sideways. Deep sleep during the day lasts for five or ten minutes at a time, and I have found that during most of that period the eyes are three-quarters shut. Occasionally they open for a few seconds, as when dozing, but soon almost close again. With care you can approach very close to these sleeping hares, if no other wild creature is near to raise the alarm.

When hares waken after sleeping soundly, they usually stretch themselves fully, as a dog does, then hop a few paces and begin to feed. Near or beside the entrance to a burrow there is usually a well-worn flat spot where they rest; moulted fur trodden into the mud or peat makes a comfortable covering. Some also have forms in the heather, somewhat similar to those of brown hares in long grass. Hares occupying these forms can usually be spotted from a distance, but I have seen them leave their forms and wriggle and push in among the surrounding long heather stems until they were completely hidden, even from above. This habit provides one reason why accurate estimates of hare densities cannot be made; such well-concealed animals normally bolt only if you are about to step on them.

It is often said that hares rest by day and feed by night, but on Choinneachain Hill they fed vigorously during most of the day in winter, and for long daylight periods in spring and autumn. At any one time, if not disturbed, at least half of those in sight would be feeding. They eat chiefly heather, but I have frequently watched them feeding on the soft rush (*Juncus effusus*) and on the heath rush (*J. squarrosus*). In winter and spring, when there is little greenery on the hill apart from mosses, the leaves of the heath rush remain green and the hares graze them close to the ground, though they do not eat the withered fruit-bearing stems. In the corrie of Allt Choinneachain these two rushes are plentiful. The soft rush forms tall tufts which protrude through deep snow and supply food for hares when all other vegetation is covered; and the basal leaves of the heath rush form low spreading green tufts which they graze as soon as the snow melts. In winter and spring I also saw them eat green blaeberry shoots and a species of moss. Indeed, a hare will eat almost any plant and, in times of deep snow, can be a menace in a forestry plantation.

Elsewhere I have seen them use snow-drifts to surmount deer-fences and wander up and down rows of seedlings, snipping off the leading shoots, thereby causing later distortion of the trees' growth. When feeding in winter, they clear the vegetation of snow by a rapid paddling motion of the forefeet, and similarly beat down snow-covered plant tips on to patches already cleared and grazed. After feeding, they often groom themselves. Sitting up on their hind-legs, they repeatedly lick their forepaws and wash their faces in the manner of a cat; they also lick their fur and comb it with their teeth and claws.

Hares are not territorial, but they share with others a 'home range' on hillside or corrie; so, although they are not gregarious, several are often found grazing close together. If one encroaches too closely on another, a squabble sometimes develops; it will strike out with a forepaw, warning the other away. This behaviour suggests strongly that 'individual distance' is observed – as, for example, among the gregarious red deer and many species of bird. The home range of a hare often covers a narrow strip running up or down a hillside or corrie; and it does not generally leave this unless hunted or otherwise frightened or, in severe winters, driven out by starvation. I have several times seen hares make the 400-yds. crossing of the frozen Loch Turret in both directions for no obvious reason, when exposed vegetation extended far up the hillside from both shores of the loch. Possibly they were 'exploring' country not normally accessible to them, or looking for mates. I also found that the home range of certain hares with which I became familiar during frequent visits extended up a hillside without reaching the ridge. These animals invariably doubled back on their tracks and ran downhill again when they reached a particular height, readily identified by conspicuous boulders.

A pair of golden eagles regularly hunted this region, and several times I watched them from about half a mile away as they soared above the ridge. The hares in sight did not appear unduly alarmed, even when exposed in their white coats on open snow-free ground. Instead of dashing for the cover of their burrows or among rocks, they crouched and remained quite still. Such inactivity was probably their safest course; I did not see one being taken. There are also foxes on the hill, though they are well controlled by keepers; and I once saw a peregrine. Some hares are shot, but otherwise the chief factor noticeably affecting their numbers seems to be food shortage during and after prolonged snow-storms. Ten days after one exceptionally severe storm, when heavy drifting occurred, I came on six fresh carcasses in the course of a two-mile walk.

HEDGEHOGS

The Pipes of Pan by Joan Blewitt Cox
For some days we had been puzzled by a high-pitched piping or whistling note in the garden. It was a peculiar, penetrating noise, that seemed to be everywhere. Late one evening, as I returned home in the dark, I heard it again, very insistent and seeming louder than ever in the silence of the night. By the time I had fetched a torch it had stopped, but I began a careful search of the garden. Suddenly, right at my feet, the noise started again and the light of my torch showed a mother hedgehog having trouble with a young one, which apparently had fallen down the rockery wall and was unable to climb up again. It failed to get a firm grip on the stones, as its mother was able to do, and kept falling backwards. It had evidently grown too large for its mother to carry it in the usual manner, rolled up underneath her, although she tried

(above) *Dartmoor pony in full coat near Widdecombe-in-the-Moor;* (below) *Palomino mare and foal near Windermere*

(above) *Long-tailed field mouse or wood mouse – eating only
the tiny seeds from the berries and discarding the juicy parts;*
(below) *house mouse on the alert*

several times. The only other way she could help was to push her nose under it, manoeuvre it on her back and give it a heave up the wall. Unfortunately, every time she lifted the young one, her spines stuck into its soft little belly and caused it to squeal. Knowing that the human voice can have a reassuring effect on animals, I spoke softly to the mother, which stood calmly by, as I placed her offspring safely on top of the wall, where she immediately followed. The pair then walked off, the baby gambolling at the mother's side. Since that night there has been no more piping, so I can only conclude that the old hedgehog had been trying to get the young one up the rockery for several days.

Pale and Dark   by Raymond Hewson

Two hedgehogs, I thought, would control the hordes of slugs which devoured annuals, perennials and the soft growth of shrubs in my walled garden. A friend brought them one July. One, pale-spined, slightly Roman-nosed, weighed a pound and a half; the other, darker, more alert, two ounces less. They moved quickly round the garden and squeezed out through an improbably small gap under the gate. When I nailed a board across the gap, they dug soil from between the cobble-stones in an attempt to burrow under it; but after a few days they stopped trying to escape. I was surprised at their digging ability.

Initially both remained in cover. Dark established a day-time resting place under a Lenten rose; Pale chose *Anemone japonica*

near old wall-trained trees about twelve yards away. These and all subsequent nest sites were at the foot of a south-facing wall, though equally good cover was to be found under others. The summer nests were flimsy – no more than scratched-out hollows lined with leaves. Each hedgehog kept to his own except when Pale's was destroyed by the dog; he then shared Dark's Lenten rose. After a few days the dog ceased to worry them, though she did make an abortive attempt to tunnel under one that was asleep.

Before emerging from the nest each would scratch himself for several minutes, and the sound was clearly audible ten or more yards away. They used well-worn trails among the shrubs, often keeping near walls; and when I dug over a border they avoided the uneven ground, joining the original trail where the digging ended. The last section to the summer-house where they were fed seemed disproportionately worn, until I found that soil adhering to their feet was trodden on to the grass, plastering it down, suppressing and finally killing it.

In the evening, as they searched the lawn for worms, they moved more quickly and stood higher on their legs than in the more commonly seen rather furtive creep. Dark scratched at crumbling lime-mortar and excavated the soil at the foot of the wall, sniffing like a hunting dog, probably in search of woodlice. Off the lawn, when hunting, both moved noisily with the slow shuffling progress familiar to anyone who has heard a hedgehog in a spinney or hedge-bottom.

Three weeks after their arrival one followed me into the summer-house to be fed, and thereafter they turned up regularly each evening. Usually they shared amicably the one dish, but sometimes they quarrelled. One evening they were working the north side of the garden and moving towards the summer-house, when one appeared to thrust his shoulder against the hind quarters of the other several times and gave a series of snuffling grunts. Both then moved round in a tight circle, as if manoeuvring to attack. Red stains on one hedgehog next morning may have been blood from this encounter. On another occasion, when feeding, one turned on the other, grunting, and appeared to be trying to push spines into him. Blood-stains at thigh and shoulder accorded with this type of behaviour. A third encounter ended without violence, perhaps because the heavier animal had established dominance, and no further fighting was seen. Something about this behaviour seemed familiar, and I found that twenty years earlier I had made a note that a hedgehog found wandering at night gave 'a little coughing bark' and 'jumped slightly', frightening my dog. At close quarters the 'slight jump' was probably the jerky spine-thrusting movement, which might also have alarmed a predator.

My original purpose in acquiring the hedgehogs had been slug control; but if, as the 'Handbook of British Mammals' suggests, one normally forages over several acres, two in a garden occupying

91

a sixteenth of an acre were too many. Despite regular but varied experimental feeding, both developed symptoms of starvation, with convulsions; my wife had to revive them with raw egg and minced steak. Thereafter they got bigger and less varied meals, preferring bread and milk to meat; they were fond of chocolate cake. A young sparrow several days dead was quickly eaten, but only the brain of a kestrel. A freshly killed mountain hare remained untouched, and I found they took a long time to deal with large pieces of meat. When Dark gnawed my fingers, I noticed that his teeth were not particularly sharp, nor his bite strong. Although I then cut meat into small pieces, they ate the bread and milk first from the same dish.

Both appeared within a few minutes of their food being put out in the evenings, and we could watch them feeding by torch-light, with their muddy feet in the dish as they made loud sucking noises. Common gull's eggs they would eat but could not break. There was no apparent reduction in the number of slugs, which they seemed to find difficult to deal with because of the slime. A large slug was pawed about, licked from end to end and bitten at both ends, before being eaten from the middle. The hedgehogs rolled others in the dust with their chins before they started to eat them. Dr E. J. Dimelow, in a study of hedgehog feeding

habits, has pointed out that some species of slug, one of which I gave them, may be unpalatable to hedgehogs because of their tough skins. The most obvious and welcome sign of foraging was the absence of worm-casts on the lawn.

Unfortunately Dark did not survive long. He wandered abroad in daylight and climbed over my shoes as I picked red currants, which he accepted from my fingers. He gnawed my shoes, sniffed at my socks and pushed his snout up my trouser-leg. Only a week or two later, when he was asleep in the open on a sunny day, did it occur to me too late that he was unwell. I should have realised that the frequent day-time appearances were abnormal, and that he was not gaining weight like his companion. The vet diagnosed an enteric infection, but the condition was then irremediable.

In the autumn Pale prepared for hibernation by adding to a summer nest in a clump of foxgloves. I put down dried bracken a few feet away because there were no tree stumps, hedge-bottoms, overgrown banks or other well-sheltered places which a wild hedgehog might have chosen. He added the material to the nest within a week. I did not construct the rather elaborate hedgehog 'nest-boxes' described in the Henry Doubleday Research Association booklet 'Operation Tiggywinkle' because I wanted to see how the animal went about things on his own account. The

garden contained shrubs, small trees and dense clumps of perennials which, with the bracken, provided nest-building material.

By late October Pale had become less active. A week later the temperature dropped to six degrees below freezing, and the north side of the garden remained frozen all day. Nothing more was added to the nest, but one night I met him going down the lane alongside the house towards the main street. I brought him back and fed him in the kitchen, after weighing him. At two pounds three ounces he was forty per cent heavier than in July, his weight having increased steadily since early August. The hibernation nest had only an inch of leaves as a covering, but in time they became compressed into a thin dense mat. March was cold and I feared that the nest was becoming thinner; but Pale appeared on a mild evening in early April, nine ounces lighter, and set off through the open garden gate on a tour of exploration.

The dog then destroyed the winter nest. Given a pile of dead leaves, Pale fashioned a new summer one in the corner of the summer-house in a single night. From here he moved back to the earlier site under the Lenten rose, emerging each evening to follow the old trails and again making a pronounced track across the lawn. He never became much tamer, though he allowed himself to be lifted without curling up. If he was alarmed when being carried, the contraction of the great back muscle was surprisingly powerful.

One night he escaped into the buildings and chose as a day-time resting place a piece of wire netting two feet square in full view in the middle of a stone floor. Feeling the wire on his spines as he pushed under it, he probably decided that he had encountered a twiggy shrub, just as (according to Derek Goodwin) feral pigeons will incorporate in their nests pieces of wire instead of twigs.

In his second winter Pale hibernated in the Lenten rose and added fresh material to a rather bulky summer nest, not unlike that of a coot. There was again no true roof - just a thin covering of leaves collected, along with a piece of plastic, from the garden. About half the leaves from a clump of *Primula denticulata* were bitten off and built into the nest. At two pounds five ounces Pale had reached a greater pre-hibernation weight than the previous year; but he lost some of it while active in the cold weather of early November.

Snow came early. Pale stayed in his nest in cold spells and came out to be fed when it was mild. In December six inches of snow fell; the nest, snow-covered, began to settle and the leaves again formed a thin mat, perhaps partly decomposing in the process. Such a mat would probably resist rain better than would a covering of loose leaves, some of which might blow away in high winds. It remained intact throughout each winter.

Drawings by Robert Gillmor

Hedgehog Road-Sense   by H. F. Barnes

I was woken about one o'clock on an August morning by a shrill noise, which might have come from some noisy little owls, a shrieking babe or a frolicsome cat. Imagine my surprise when I discovered it to be from a hedgehog and its four young, which had been born in one of the rotting leaf-heaps in our back garden. The hedgehog was vociferously escorting its offspring under our side gate. Not wishing to lose the family I took it back to the nest at the far end of the garden and blocked the space under the side gate with pieces of wood. An hour later the noise started again, and this time I waited to see what would happen. The family was now on the pavement outside the front garden. (Our house is on a corner near the centre of the town.) Instead of going straight out on to the road, the hedgehog had gone just round the corner of our front wall. After squeaking intermittently for a few minutes, it edged one of its offspring off the pavement into the gutter and proceeded, with almost continuous squeaks, to run first on one side and then on the other of the youngster, which was thus directed diagonally across the road, straight towards a gateway a short distance down the side road. As soon as the little one was safely inside this entrance to another garden, the parent scuttled silently back across the road to where its remaining young were waiting. Then, squeaking again, it edged another off the pavement and escorted it across the road in exactly the same fashion. It repeated this procedure a third and fourth time, on each occasion bringing one of its family safely across. As if to show that it could count, it did not return for a fifth, but, lowering its voice, scurried hither and thither up the garden with its family.

Prickly Invasion   by Anne Ray-Hills

On the first cold evening of autumn I thought I heard the cat at the back door and opened it. Scrambling across the floor was a baby hedgehog, no bigger than the palm of my hand. Feeling that it would die of cold outside, we put it in a cardboard box full of crumpled newspaper. During the night the cat pushed the back door open and came in. Next morning the hedgehog, having apparently climbed out of the box, was drinking milk from the cat's saucer but, when we removed the crumpled paper, our original visitor was still there. The milk thief was a brother or sister. We put them in the greenhouse and thought that was the end of the matter. During the next week we found baby hedgehogs, not all the same size, everywhere: behind the cooker, under the refrigerator, under shelves, and hidden in cupboards. The final count, as the result of the door being left open that frosty night, was eleven young ones and a large adult. They all stayed in the greenhouse until the spring, when we let them into the garden.

Hedgehog, a scraperboard by Kenneth Underwood

Our dog has since brought in two soft-spined babies, but I do not think he was the original culprit because there was no indication of fleas on him, as usually happens when he has been 'hedgehogging'.

An Inconclusive Affair   by Jeremy Lingard

The call was loud and harsh enough to be a jay, but rather too mournful and repetitive; so I thought as I crept across the wet, decaying leaves of a Hertfordshire wood on a warm, humid mid-June evening. Avoiding twigs and patches of bracken, I came to a small clearing a hundred yards from the footpath. Two hedgehogs were nose to nose, one shrieking like a jay and the other apparently sniffing, though it made a noise resembling a combination of hissing weasel, chattering vole and squeaking shrew, audible twenty yards away. It is difficult, if not impossible, to sex live and active hedgehogs, but I assumed that it was the female who was shrieking, while the male hissed and pursued her. Their movements were slow, as the female was not adept at walking backwards and there were brief pauses whenever she snapped at the male. They continued in a circle of about a yard diameter but, after about 15 minutes, the male walked away one or two yards, only to return at once and start again; two minutes later he walked five yards away, but soon returned trotting purposefully under the bracken. Since the female had made no attempt to escape, mating seemed probable but, following further sniffing, squawking and nose-to-nose shuffling, the male went away again. He seemed to have lost some enthusiasm and, after a minute or so, the female lifted a hind leg and began to scratch herself. A minute afterwards, the male appeared for the last time. The female raised her nose in his direction but, before he had time to raise his voice or get within a foot of her, she backed away with a sniff; he promptly turned his back and wandered off into the undergrowth. The female scratched briefly, then began to search for food among the dead leaves, meandering slowly into the gathering gloom.

Hedgehog Courtship   by D. F. Powell

One night in summer I heard outside my window a sharp snuffle, constantly repeated, as if a dog were on the scent of a rabbit. Soon the sound was recurring at regular intervals, too persistent and rhythmical for a dog. Looking out, I could just distinguish, on a patch of lawn dimly lit from the house, a dark moving mass that appeared to be turning round and round. I went out and found that it was a pair of hedgehogs. One was squatting in the grass, which was long and uncut here. She it was, I discovered after a long and careful observation, that emitted the loud quick snorts. Her mate was fully occupied in lumbering round and round her in a small circle. Between them, they flattened the grass nicely. As he proceeded she, small and quick in her movements, jumped round, always presenting her nose to his. And with each little jump she snorted. Neither took the slightest notice of me. I touched their backs in turn gingerly, and gazed into the male's eyes, with my nose almost touching his as he completed his circles towards me, but the pair seemed unaware of my presence. He must have been circling round with hardly a break for an hour and fifty minutes, when twice he stopped suddenly, sniffed the air and looked me curiously in the face. The first time he went off into the undergrowth, evidently suspicious, but his mate remained, unconcerned, and after a moment began to feed. Then he returned, and it began all over again. The second time he, evidently more alert than she, lumbered off once more – and without awaiting his return I went indoors.

Hedgehog Hangover   by Gabriel Barlow

Tins or jars half filled with beer will catch a lot of slugs and snails; I leave them in strategic places until they are full. One night I noticed that tins which had been half full on my previous inspection were now empty. This happened several times and I was puzzled, until I saw a hedgehog leaning over a tin, disposing of slugs, snails and beer. Oblivious of my torch he kept at it and emptied the tin, then wiped his mouth with his front paws and moved off. His progress was unsteady, and after going some way he lay on his side and curled up. An hour later he was still sleeping it off.

Bone Meal   by Josephine Swinscow

A hedgehog, walking slowly across our lawn, passed a large marrow-bone which my spaniel had left under a tree. Then it stopped, sniffed the air, turned round and went back to investigate. After circling the bone slowly several times, the hedgehog put a paw on it to steady it, before chewing away for several minutes with good appetite. The dog, watching from the window, appeared astonished and affronted to see another animal eating what he considered to be his exclusive property.

HORSES

Mettle   by Martin Wade

I was just about ready for bed when Father remarked casually that in the morning he would be taking Mettle to be shod. 'Be careful, dear,' said Mother.

Mettle was a shire, steel grey and vicious, a two-year-old going on three. She was never completely broken and had a history of runaway carts, broken shafts and harness. Her ability to turn and kick with her massive hind legs was well known. Old Dan had told me: 'She'm a bad un, as was her mother, and her mother before that, They'm fighting horses – always was. Horses like her went into battle carrying knights.' Father had warned me to keep away from her, adding: 'One of these days she'll kill somebody.'

In the morning I staggered lifelessly downstairs and collapsed in a miserable heap in the armchair. 'I have pains, Mam, all in my stomach, chest and head.'

Father came in for his meal and asked, 'What's the matter, lad?'

'He's ill,' said Mother, 'too ill to go to school.'

Away they went at a fine pace

As the school bell rang, my aches vanished miraculously. 'I feel better now, Dad. I'll go and feed the calves for you.'

'You're as bad as he is, Dad,' Mother said, as I dashed out of the door followed by Father's laughter.

The church clock struck ten, and Father went to bridle Mettle. Five minutes later the banging, squealing and bad language subsided, the stable door flew open, and Father and Mettle hurtled through in an explosion of hooves and boots. 'Keep well back,' shouted Father, as shoulder to shoulder they whirled and spun in the crew yard, scattering hysterical Rhode Island Reds and Buff Orpingtons. Bill, wheeling a load of muck across the yard, ran like a frightened rabbit to the safety of the cowshed; and Mettle in her fury sent barrow and contents spinning into the air. 'Hang on, Harry! Hang on!' shouted Horace from the safety of the pig pens.

Mettle stopped and began to kick – slowly at first, then faster and faster. Up and down, up and down, went the unshod hooves into the liquid mud and muck. The spray splashed and stained the wall of the barn, and quite saturated Father and the horse.

'Open the gate, lad,' roared Dad through mud-splattered lips, 'we're ready to go.' And away they went at a fine pace, hooves smacking at the dusty road to the smithy.

As Joe helped Father to tie Mettle to the stout ring on the smithy wall, he laughed at their muddy appearance. She allowed Joe to pick up each foot in turn and pare it with his sharp knife. Not by a flick of her tail or twitch of her ears did she betray her rage. Joe's soothing 'Steady up my old beauty', 'Whoa then' and 'Come on old gal' seemed to have worked their charm. Disappointed, I turned to look down the road; and then it happened.

Joe was the first to come flying out, with Father a close second. 'By gum, Harry, we've a wild one here.' The mare sent Joe's heavy wooden box of tools and nails hurtling across the road, followed swiftly by the iron footstool. We picked up the nails and tools, as Joe gazed ruefully at the broken box. His father had given it to him when he left school, at the age of ten, to start work at the forge. It held a deal of sentiment for him.

He tugged his heavy brown moustache; then, hammer in hand, he strode back into the smithy, where he stood for a moment looking at Mettle. She turned her head to size him up, shifting from leg to leg, and kicked. Had Joe been a foot nearer, it would have been the end of him. The hoof hung for a brief second in front of him. With a roar of anger, he dropped his hammer and seized the leg. 'So you want to shake hands, do you? Come on then. I'll shake hands with you – any time.'

Tied to the stout ring on the smithy wall

I don't know who was most surprised: Mettle, my father or I. Joe hung on grimly. Beads of sweat ran down his face. Backwards and forwards he swayed, as Mettle struggled to retrieve her leg. She hopped on her free one and tried to steady herself enough to let fly with that too.

'Give me the other too, if you like. I'll teach you to smash my box.'

Mettle hopped again and Joe, with a superhuman heave, sent her crashing on her side to the floor of the smithy in a cloud of dust.

She lay there for a moment before scrambling to her feet. Afterwards Father said that she weighed well over a ton, and Joe must have lifted at least half of that. His strength spent for the moment, Joe sat down and wiped the sweat from his face with a large spotted handkerchief. Father was the first to speak: 'I've never seen anything like that in my life.'

'Neither have I,' said Joe; and they both laughed.

I picked up his broken box and carried it to him. 'It's not badly broken, Joe. You can soon mend it.'

'Ay, that I can, lad, that I can.' And the ham-like hand that had done the mighty deed patted me gently on the head.

After that things were pretty tame. A few times Mettle tried to crush Joe against the wall by leaning on him. She would have bitten him as he bent over her forelegs, but Father was holding her head and prevented her. By noon she was complete with a full set of shoes. As she left the forge, the metal crashing and striking against the cobbled floor, she aimed a side-ways kick at Joe, slipped and almost came a cropper again.

'Serve you darned well right.' And Joe called after Father: 'Don't be in a hurry to bring her again, Harry'.

The children were just coming out of school. 'Best slip home the back way, through the farm and across the paddock,' Dad advised. So I was the first to tell Mother how Joe, the mighty blacksmith, had lifted a shire horse above his head and thrown her to the ground.

Drawings by Joan Begbie

A Friend in Greed   by Barbara de Seyssel

Alice was a large carthorse whose only serious fault was greed. Anything, she seemed to think, was worth a try, from hen food, well trampled and several days old, to the blacksmith's braces, which she insisted on sampling to the full extent of the elastic as he bent over her fore-foot, helpless, his mouth full of nails. Delia was a nondescript brown hen who spent the day round the stables and roosted at night above the harness racks, if she got the chance. One morning when I gave the mare her oats, Delia was up in the manger and looked as if she was about to lay, so I went off to milk, determined to hurry back, because eggs were not plentiful then. On my return Delia was scratching as usual in the straw under Alice, who was pulling hay from the rack. Among the debris of the hay I could see the distinct form of the nest, which was still warm, but there was no egg.

Two mornings later I again found Delia sitting, and again there was no trace of an egg. So, on the third occasion, after I had fed Alice I retired to the adjoining stall and kept watch through a handy knot-hole at eye· level. The mare amused herself by chasing the remains of her breakfast into corners, but I noticed that she kept an eye on the hen who was sitting at my end of the manger. Once or twice she nosed up close; then she blew on the hen, ruffling her feathers. Delia sat tight, however, until Alice without warning tipped her sideways, only to get a sharp peck which made her withdraw and rub her nose on the manger. Delia settled down again and Alice sighed, her lower lip hanging down, and dribbled a little. Suddenly, without a sound, Delia stood up and stretched; there between her legs was an egg. I made a dash round the partition, only to find Alice's great quarters swung over against me, and it was a second or two before I could squeeze up to the manger, where I found her holding her head high. As I reached up, the yolk of the egg ran down my arm.

The Medieval Great Horse   by H. Bourne

All modern heavy breeds of horses, in England and on the Continent, are descended from a single stock – the Great Horse of the Middle Ages, which alone was capable of carrying a heavily-armoured warrior on the battlefield, and so was bred and developed throughout that period for the specific purpose. This horse had to be able to carry up to four hundredweight, to charge and to stand the terrific shock of meeting in full career an opponent of equal weight and power. He was always a stallion, for only a stallion would have the strength to bear such a weight, and the courage to charge fearlessly under such conditions. (Mares were used only for breeding.) Black seems to have been the most usual colour. Picture a stallion of the heaviest type you know, coal-black, with a great crested neck, and of a fiery temper, armoured with steel plates like a tank, and bearing a rider completely encased in steel, and you will have some idea of the awe with which the common people regarded the knightly warrior.

At that date all menial labour was performed by oxen, and the breeding and ownership of the Great Horse were the prerogatives of the nobility. In time of peace he carried his master amid the splendid pageantry of the tournament. In war the fate of the nation depended on him. Trapped in velvet and adorned with gold and jewels, he bore conquering princes in their triumph; kings rode upon him to receive the homage of their vassals; and the knights-errant saluted their ladies from his back. But then the invention of gunpowder and the introduction of fire-arms rendered the shock-charge of the heavily armoured knights ineffective and obsolete. The new military tactics demanded mobility, for which a lighter type of horse was more suitable. So the Great Horse fell from his high position.

Some Fine Old Business   by Charles Bowness

'Harness Tulip,' said Nat, 'and me and Teni and Charlie can be off to see about buying some gryas.' As Teni obediently sorted the harness from where it hung on the rear of the trolley, I fetched the mare, raised the shafts and backed her into them. Teni winked at me across her back.

'You'll see some fine old business soon, brother.' He nodded to where Nat stood talking to some friends. 'The best gryengro on the drom.'

Old Nat was one of those who formed within the travellers a respected confident freemasonry of horse-dealers. Skilled at staying on the right side of the law, their success depended on a fraternal sharing of trade secrets and their individual intelligence.

'Hop up,' said Teni, and we jumped on the trolley.

He shook the reins, and Tulip took the strain easily, using her strength wisely. She arched her neck in a familiar pride at drawing a vehicle, ears twitching and eyes big and bold. When she had stretched her legs, she paced herself into a rhythmic canter, her long black tail flowing like a proud banner. There was only one small hill to climb and, when we reached it, the shoulders of the black mare slipped forward under the smooth skin as she laid back her ears and stretched out her neck for balance. At the summit she settled her quarters into the breeching and went slowly down the other side.

At the old Wold farmhouse, at the foot of the hill, a middle-aged man in breeches and stockings walked across to meet us.

Stepping forward, Nat extended his hand. 'Good morning, Mr Wallis.'

'How do, Mr Lee.' The farmer's speech was quiet and deliberate, and he gave us all a slow smile.

We walked about half a mile to a paddock A brown gelding, obviously past his prime, stood quietly by a pollard willow almost in the centre of the field. Near him stood a grey colt, gazing suspiciously, ears twitching.

'Can't do much with that colt,' observed the farmer, putting a foot on a bar of the gate. 'If you hadn't come, I was getting a breaker in to him next week.'

Nat looked at the animals without enthusiasm 'If he ain't broken, he ain't a lot of use to us.' He took his pipe from his pocket. 'And the other one ain't getting any younger.'

The farmer handed him a box of matches: 'Neither are you, but he'll last you out.'

'Maybe,' replied Nat with a grin, 'but nobody's thinking of buying me.'

Mr Wallis laughed. 'Well, there they are. It's up to you. Have a good look at them, and you'll find they're worth a fair price.'

Nat gave a nod to Teni, and the young gypsy vaulted the gate and walked towards the horses. The colt started in alarm, tossed his head and trotted a few yards farther away to watch warily as

Teni approached his companion. Teni put his arm round the rigid thickness of the gelding's lower neck. For a moment he appeared to be talking to the horse; then, placing his hand through the head-stall, he led him slowly towards us. Nat opened the horse's mouth and grunted non-committally. Passing his hand over side and quarter, he gave a disapproving sniff. Then he lifted each leg in turn and muttered incomprehensible words.

'I've never see'd such an ignorant-looking horse, brother.'

Mr Wallis looked slightly annoyed. 'What's wrong with him?'

'First place,' said Nat, 'he'll be going lame any day now. Badly shod.'

'No!' said the farmer in disbelief. 'Why, I've always thought our blacksmith was pretty good.'

'You might, Mr Wallis,' replied Nat drily, 'but next time you see him, tell him from me it's best to make the shoe fit the horse, not the horse fit the shoe. He's filed enough off them hooves to feed all the sick dogs in London. He's ruining that horse's feet; they're as dry as bone. No oil left in 'em.'

The farmer looked a bit disconcerted, then rallied his business sense. 'Tell you what, Mr Lee, I'll let you have him for sixty guineas.'

Nat laughed loudly. 'I'll say this for you, Mr Wallis, you likes a joke.' Assuming a serious expression again, he studied the pipe in his hand. 'Now I couldn't buy that horse from you – all my pals would laugh – but we've been friends for a long time now, so I'll give you a bit of advice. You take him along to Brigg Fair. You might get sixty guineas after the pubs have closed, if it's dark enough.'

'Say fifty guineas?'

'Mr Wallis,' said Nat, 'I wouldn't say yes to forty.'

'Name your price then.'

Nat seemed to be about to speak, but Teni caught his eye and shook his head solemnly.

'There you are,' the old gypsy said, 'I was going to say thirty-nine guineas, but my lad don't want me to buy. He's a better judge of horses than I am.'

'What will you give me for him?' asked the farmer a trifle impatiently.

'Thirty-five.'

'Make it thirty-eight.'

'It's a deal,' cried Nat, raising his right arm.

The farmer took his hand, 'Right.'

'Now,' said Nat comfortably, 'what about the other?'

Grinning, Mr Wallis said, 'If you can catch him.'

'My lad will catch him.'

Teni released the gelding and walked slowly to the centre of the field and stood there with his hands on his hips like a bull-fighter weighing up his foe. The colt pricked up his ears and opened his nostrils wide. Teni went a little closer. The stallion stood in a nervous agony of suspense, a tremor running along his spine. So suddenly that it made me jump, he tossed his head, uttered a shrill cry of warning to himself and pawed the earth in gathering rage. I glanced at Nat.

'Dordi,' he said, 'he's a bad 'un.'

The horse lowered his head as if to make a close inspection, while Teni walked steadily nearer. Then, in a temporary end to his struggle between fear and hate, the colt gave a fierce neigh and turned swiftly aside, tail arched, and galloped round the perimeter of the field.

'Head him off!' called Teni.

Nat and I scrambled over the gate and flapped our arms as the horse came round for the second time. He swerved and thundered by us, flanks darkened by the sweat of incipient panic. Teni began to run ahead of the colt, who was coming up alongside, and was reaching with his hands when he stumbled and fell. The horse turned and slithered in a short circle before the gypsy was half risen, neighed defiantly, then rose on his hind legs, swinging his tail.

'My God!' exclaimed Nat in a choked voice. He sprinted across the field with me at his heels. The stallion, swiftly rejecting the original hot impulse, turned and his hind legs shot out as he galloped off at speed. A clod of earth and grass shot over our heads and pattered through the leaves of the trees like shrapnel. Teni lay on the ground, writhing in pain.

'Caught me on the leg,' he gritted through strained lips.

'Thank God it wasn't your head,' said the farmer.

The grey colt stood in the corner of the paddock, nostrils quivering and eyes bloodshot. Still near the gate, the gelding watched with patient shyness. We gently carried Teni to the cart.

'I'll phone for the doctor,' suggested Mr Wallis.

'No,' protested Teni, 'most of the pain has gone now. The horse only just caught me.'

'He'll be coming back up here for that colt in three days' time,' predicted Nat, kneeling on a couple of sacks to conclude his examination. 'His leg ain't broken.'

'Is there anything I can do?' asked the farmer.

Teni rolled down his trouser-leg, covering the enormous bruise which had begun to appear below his knee. 'I could do with a cigarette.'

The colour returned to the farmer's cheeks as his anxiety lessened. Soon we left him. Nat pulled a cigarette from behind his ear and handed it to Teni: 'All right, lad?'

'Yes, I'll be all right.' He gave me a wry grin. 'Afore the week is out I'll be off back for them two gryas, and there won't be any nonsense about it next time.'

'Just a bit of bad luck,' commented Nat. He gave me a sidelong glance. 'We'll be sure to get the colt cheap now.'

Blackmail by Leslie Anderson

When I was postman in rural Lincolnshire, I was met regularly at one farm gate by two high-spirited ponies who would allow my small van through only after much persuasion and offerings of sweets. In return, the van was thoroughly examined, windscreens and bodywork lovingly cleaned over.

All went well until the day I forgot the sweets. With a lot of extra fussing I got the van through and the gate safely closed; but having delivered the mail I realised that the ponies were escorting me all round the farmstead in expectation of their reward. Back at the gate they stood quietly broadside, blocking my exit.

Time pressed, for I had hardly begun my round. Soft words proving futile, I tried sterner ones, then shooing and shoving and finally chasing. They got the message and stood well clear while I reopened the gate and got into the van; then one of them dashed out and was off down the lane to the main road.

Back I had to go to the house and confess to the farmer. He looked over my shoulder and out across his land, then laughed. To my great relief the pony was already trotting back, whinnying merrily. I did not forget the candies again.

MICE

Tale of Three Mice   by Florence Miller

I caught a nearly full-grown long-tailed field mouse in my pantry one February. He was dark brown on the back, warmer at the sides, shading almost to chestnut, with white underparts, and I called him Persil. (I always thought of him as male.) After he had gnawed at every crack in a wooden cage, I put him in a large tin-lined cage with glass front. The roof had a small trapdoor and was lined with perforated zinc.

Persil seemed to be short-sighted, for he came to study me at the glass when I stood close to it; but the moment I put my hand through the trapdoor he smelt me and shot into bed. He could jump almost a foot straight upwards, and climb up and down a length of very thin twine; he also liked to run about upside-down on the perforated zinc ceiling. His diet included bread, biscuit, cheese, milk puddings and especially custard, various seeds and berries, cooked potatoes and carrots; also small animals, particularly spiders and caterpillars. He would eat carrots raw in my pantry, but turned up his nose at them, unless cooked, when he had other food in his cage.

Two half-grown house mice invaded my home in November and looked so comical as they whisked and frisked about the dining-room that I decided to keep them and compare their behaviour with that of the field mouse. A Heath-Robinson trap – a tall narrow-necked jug with a thin strip of wood balanced on the edge – soon caught both, and they grew tame enough to snatch titbits from my fingers. But I had to take care, because they too were able to jump nearly a foot upwards and threatened to gnaw their way out of a wooden cage. So I decided to put them in the tin-lined cage with Persil. He slept in one corner of it, in a small open-topped box filled with hay: this had two entrance holes at floor level.

I made a similar bed in the opposite corner and dropped the 'twins' into it. They dived under the hay, but soon reappeared to begin exploring. At first they stopped short of Persil's bedroom, but after a few days they would scamper across, poke their noses in the entrance and dash off again, like naughty boys banging on a door-knocker. In the ensuing weeks the twins and Persil spent much time each evening snatching bits of each other's hay and taking it into their beds. Then one morning one bed was empty, the other crammed with hay, and all three mice were sleeping in it; and there they stayed. Persil went in and out of bed through the entrance holes, but the twins normally popped up and down through the hay.

All three did acrobatics on a sloping branch and ran upside-down on the ceiling. The twins often leapt into the air with front legs wide apart, bringing their 'hands' together at the top of the jump, to close on either side of a thin twig, along which they then ran upside-down. When they leapt up to the roof they would turn in mid air and arrive feet first; when they dropped, they always fell on their feet. If I put a hand in the cage the twins froze where they were, unless I came too close, when they would dash into bed. Persil always rushed to bed if danger threatened, to stay motionless until I touched him; then he would shoot out of the other

Whisky, Frisky and Persil by Robert Gillmor

entrance and across to the bed opposite, which they used as a
lavatory. If the twins were in bed and I poked my finger in, they
bit it. They were usually together, often side by side on the bedroom wall washing each other.

Soon after the twins had become full-grown, I left the trapdoor
open for a moment and Frisky popped out. I recaptured him rather
more than a week later and dropped him back into the cage. To
my surprise he hesitated outside the bedroom, then scampered
about the cage until Whisky poked his head up through the hay.
He sprang down and flew at Frisky, who fled. Up and down the
cage, in and out of the bedroom they rushed, knocking Persil over
in their wild chase. I hurriedly inserted my hand, and Whisky
dived into bed where Persil was now cowering; but Frisky fell on
the floor exhausted. I lifted him out and he lay panting on my
hand, bleeding from so many bites that I had to put him out of his
misery.

112

Whisky was feeding quietly soon afterwards, as if nothing had happened; but Persil was staggering to the water and gulped down a lot before crawling into bed. He was dead in the morning, without apparent injury. I think the excitement must have been too much for him. Whisky got more and more bad-tempered, sitting on the branch and twitching his tail when I cleaned the cage. Soon he became so vicious that I had to part with him.

Baited   by M. W. Graham

The head ploughman was having his bait one early spring morning when I took a message out to him. Beside him lay an old overcoat which had long seen better days. As we talked, a mouse popped up on the collar of the coat, disappeared and re-emerged at the sleeve cuff. It then ran underneath the full length of the coat, surfacing bright-eyed at each button-hole, and finally, to judge by the moving hump under the coat, returned to base at the collar. The ploughman stretched out his hand with a fragment of sandwich, ' 'Ere, mate,' he said, ' 'ave a go at this.' Quicker than the eye could follow, the mouse snatched the titbit and was gone.

Homing Mouse   by Jane Craik

On a cold March morning I found a bedraggled long-tailed field mouse in my Longworth mammal trap, set in a garden shed where mice had been raiding a sack of potatoes. It appeared to be dead, but soon recovered in a basket before the fire. A damaged tail made future identification easy. That evening I released it with two other mice on the moor outside the garden gate. In the morning, to my surprise, Tommy (as I named him) was back on the trap in the shed. Although I liberated him in various directions, at increasing distances of up to 500 yds. from the gate, he always returned to the trap within a few days. By the end of May it was evident that

Tommy should have been called Thomasina, but I changed only the pronoun. One day, when placed in a hamster cage, she seemed forlorn and wandered aimlessly around until I put the outer portion of the Longworth trap into the cage. Her reaction was instantaneous; here was the ideal nestbox, a flat-sided container, $5\frac{1}{2}$ in. long and closed at one end. Losing no time, she gathered hay and scraps of newspaper from the floor of the cage, filling the nest to overflowing. Finally she vanished inside for two days. On the third evening she came out for food, leaving five red, hairless, sausage-like creatures, each about the size of a finger-nail. Two weeks later they had grown hair, their eyes were opening, and they followed their mother on wobbly legs. Before they were a month old they could wriggle between the bars of the cage; so I took mother and family, with nest, out of the cage and put them by the now empty potato sack in the shed. I set no more traps there and have not seen Tommy since.

Labour-Saving by Margaret Hart

My daughter keeps her pet mouse in a glass-fronted cage with two storeys. Upstairs is a nesting compartment at the back and a ledge in front; between this and the glass there is a gap of about a sixth of an inch. The floor of the cage is covered in wood shavings, and one day the mouse came to take some for its nest. Instead of carrying them up the runway, it chose shavings near the glass, picked up one at a time in its mouth, stood on its hind legs and pushed the shaving with its front paws from its mouth, through the gap and on to the ledge. It seemed very upset if one missed the target and fell down. When it had put about a dozen shavings on the ledge, it went upstairs and dragged them the few steps to its nest. It repeated the process until it had enough bedding, thus saving itself many journeys up and down the runway.

Nutmanship by G. E. Young

One winter soon after we moved to Minehead, a large mouse took up residence in a pile of branches on the far side of our 6-ft. willow

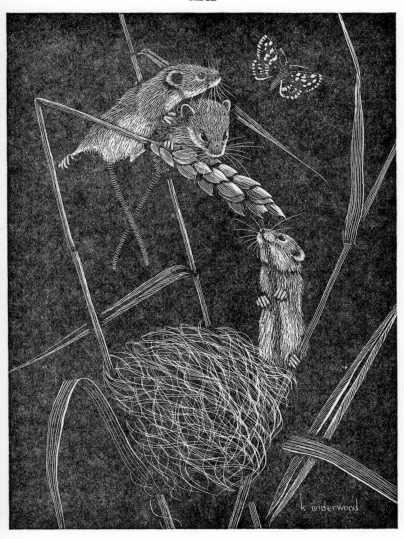

Harvest mice, a scraperboard by Kenneth Underwood

wattle fence, which is about 9 ft. from the kitchen window. To attract titmice we hung three wire rings, on which were threaded peanuts in their shells, round the tops of uprights in the fence. One night a number of nuts disappeared, so we fixed an iron shelf-bracket for each ring, hanging them from the brackets on short loops of wire. As nuts still vanished, we put a piece of stout fencing

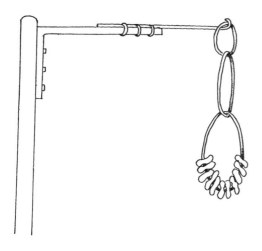

wire along the top of each bracket and hung the loops on these, so that the rings projected 6 in. farther from the fence. More nuts went, and at last my wife saw the mouse run up the wattles, along the bracket and wire, to which it hung by its hind legs, reaching forward with its forepaws to hold the ring steady while it bit out a nut. We foiled it by hanging the ring on a second loop of wire so that the mouse could no longer reach down to it and had to content itself with fragments picked up below. But in early spring a second, darker mouse appeared, bolder and more active than the first: it used to spring from the fence on to the nut rings, bite off a number in their shells, let them fall, then follow them by dropping some 5 ft. to the ground.

[The size, activity and diurnal behaviour of the mice strongly suggest that they were yellow-necked rather than the commoner wood mice. *B.C.*]

Covered Up   by H. Finlay

On moving to a country cottage, we found many mice in the garage (a former coach-house) and in the loft, where there was fibre-glass for insulation. We had no animals and felt it was safe to place small dishes of warfarin at several points. To our surprise we found those in the loft neatly covered with tufts of fibre-glass, and those in the coal-shed with minute pieces of coal and wood; the garage dishes were under a layer of dry leaves. Meanwhile we had caught several mice in cheese traps, and there was no sign of another for some weeks.

[When trapping for small mammals, I usually put traps in pairs; and in the autumn it is quite common to find that wood mice have fed from one and stuffed the other with twigs and bits of soil. This seems connected with their habit of hoarding. *H. N. Southern.*

MOLES

Moles on the Farm   by Richard Stileman

Countrymen have long wondered why the numbers of moles vary so much from field to field, and it has been commonly suggested that they depend on marked variations in the abundance of earthworms, the main source of food. The results of some recent research, carried out over twenty fields at Whitehouse in west Aberdeenshire, suggest that farming practice may also influence first the colonisation of fields by moles and then the build-up of their population. None of the fields on which the research was carried out had been trapped for moles for six years, and their soil and drainage were essentially similar. Sixteen had been under grass for between one and five years; the other four carried a crop of oats in 1967 and were covered during the study by a thin growth of previously undersown grass. Most of the work consisted of comparing populations within the different fields: the numbers present were counted, and the body-weights, ages and rate of mole-hill production were measured for all the moles in the area. These proved to be much more common in fields which had been under grass for at least three to five years than in those under grass for only one or two. Surprisingly the highest density was in fields undersown earlier in the year. The heaviest moles came from this group, and they had made most molehills. The lightest were in fields with only a few present, and they were also the least active in producing molehills. These were all indications that the moles were able to find more to eat in the oldest and most recent pastures than in the intermediate ones. The oldest might have been expected to harbour most moles, as it is known that mechanical cultivation often reduces the worm population drastically, and that it increases again with the years any field is in pasture. But why were there so many moles in the undersown fields, and why should their numbers fall so steeply in the year after undersowing? The answers seem to be related to the compactness of the soil. In some fields this changes considerably from year to year; soil is loose and pliable after one or more years of mechanical cultivation, but soon consolidates with the combined effects of weather and grazing, thus presumably making tunnelling more arduous. An experiment did show that moles dug more rapidly and easily in the loose soils of the undersown fields than in the much more compact older pastures. Therefore, although there may be fewer worms in the loose soils, they can be more efficiently cropped by the moles, who are then able to build up their own numbers. Heavy grazing on undersown fields may not begin until the spring following the year of sowing, and often coincides with the decline of the mole population. So it is fair to suggest that trampling of the relatively soft soil may result in the destruction of tunnels, causing the moles to desert their homes. These fields are left with few or no moles for a year or so, but are gradually recolonised. The new arrivals burrow first from the ditches and rough patches round the edges, and slowly extend their tunnels outwards to the centre of the field.

MONKEYS

Mere Monkeys   by Bhabani Bhattacharya

I stood in the doorway of the thatched house at dawn. The grey-brown mother monkey, common enough in our Central Indian villages, had come first as usual. With one arm she clasped to her fur-coat bosom her baby, perhaps a week old, as she climbed slowly and cautiously to a low branch of the tall tamarind, which was heavy with fruit. There she sat very still, giving suck and uttering a fond cry once in a while as she gazed down at the baby. Presently a dozen other monkeys came and dashed up the rugged bark of the tree. They flung out their arms towards the baby as it fed, and each snatched at it and fondled and held it, uttering a screech of joy or a gurgle in the throat. Though they jostled with one another for a turn, they were cautious and careful with the baby. When all the others had nursed it, the mother begged it back and started to give suck again; her wild amber eyes were soft as the gazed down at it and, if the pinched orb of the face of a monkey can smile, she smiled.

So it had been for the past three days. There was no accounting why the mother monkey came to this particular tamarind in the front yard of the mud-brick house, came only at the hour of dawn, gave suck and departed, and why at once the other monkeys left too. But today they were not grouped together; they sat on the outspread of the tree, very quiet, with a timid downpour of tails. The mother monkey no longer gave suck, and sat heedful, as though poised for flight the baby pressed close under her loins. Then I saw an enormous male of the species, curved tail hoisted, approaching the tamarind. He felt its trunk with his paws, then jerked round suddenly and prowled off with an air of disinterest. The strain seemed to ease; a dozen monkey faces grew less tense. The drooping tails lifted, as though all were controlled by a single nervous system.

Suddenly the huge beast turned and came back at a swift run. The monkeys trembled and sat spellbound, and in an instant the male was up on the tree, crouching before the mother and glaring at her. A long arm shot out. With a strangled cry she shielded the baby with her body, but she seemed limp with fear, and the big darting paw gripped and snatched the baby away in a single motion, flung it playfully in the air and let it drop. The helpless mother burst forth in a whooping sort of wail. It had all happened very quickly and, for me, quite unexpectedly. I threw a stone chip at the male. With teeth bared and face red with fury he came rushing down the tree and stood glaring at me, as if ready to charge. I picked up brickbats and looked round for a stick. He hesitated, then turned and bounded away out of sight.

A chorus of pathetic broken wailing now filled the air. The monkeys gathered at the foot of the tree, circling round the tiny body which reddened the mother's bosom as she held it in her arms. All wailed together and beat their breasts with their paws, making lamentation in the manner of village women. When I walked towards the group, they were at once quiet. The mother lifted up the bundle for me to see. It was as though her eyes implored and hoped, and all the other monkeys' eyes implored and hoped too. But the tender skin of the belly had burst; there was nothing to be done. As I moved away, the cries of anguish started once more. Presently the animals were gone, having taken the corpse with them. Perhaps I should never see them again.

So I thought as I came out of the house at daybreak next morning with the image of the mourners sharp in my mind and looked around. But there they were, coming at the set moment, slow-footed and utterly silent. They did not rush up the tree, but grouped themselves on the spot where the baby had hit the earth and died. First the mother began to wail, sitting on her haunches, slightly stooped, her face bowed. Then the others followed. Like professional mourners who, in this part of India, for a small fee rend the air with their ritual of full-throated wailing when someone has died, they raised shrill monkey voices, swaying on their haunches and beating their breasts.

page 121
(above) *Pygmy glider cleaning its tail (see page 136)*;
(below) *long-tailed field mouse with damaged tail and young*

Buster, the wild rabbit (see page 138)

OTTERS

Otters' Fare by the Sea   by Dugald Macintyre

Once, when I was out with a lobster-fisher of Mull setting creels, we saw an otter which was engaged with a large lobster on a tangle-fringed islet of rock. The otter plunged into the sea as we drew near, leaving its prey. Part of the lobster's shell had been stripped, and its flesh gnawed. The fisherman had never before seen an otter take a lobster, but I have several times found the remains of otter-killed lobsters on beaches in south Argyll. From my own fishing boat, looking shoreward on the west coast of Kintyre, I once saw an otter eating a large sea-trout on a shelf of rock. It plunged into the sea with the fish but, when I came closer, dropped it in deepish water. I could see the fine five-pounder lying on its side, but failed to retrieve it with the boat-hook, so I pulled away and from a distance saw the otter carry its prize out of the water to another rock, where I left it to dine in peace. In west Argyll wrasse are plentiful among the tangle, and the otters have these fish on their menus two or three times a week. They are also fond of plaice and flounders, and occasionally take sea-birds. I saw one retrieving an adult gannet to the rocks near the Mull of Kintyre, and another brought ashore a black-headed gull.

The otters of the sea-coast ascend the rivers seasonally: when food is scarce in salt water they try fresh for a change, and appreciate a bit of salmon all the more because they so seldom get any. They do not hesitate to attack large conger eels. In Kintyre a farmer who was carting wrack stopped at my door one winter day to show me a large otter which he had killed with his 'graipe', a three-pronged instrument used for throwing the seaweed on the cart. He had watched the otter and a conger fight furiously, and the otter was so exhausted when at last it dragged the big eel ashore that it fell an easy victim. A heap of hundreds of limpet-shells under a large boulder on the west coast of Mull once excited my curiosity. At first I thought of rats, but the tracks of an otter on the sand near by revealed the identity of the collector.

The most surprising action of an otter which I remember was a raid on the wrapped food of a picnic party on Mull. After lunch the left-overs were carefully covered to preserve them from the gulls. Some hours later, when two ladies of the party came back to boil the kettle for tea, what they described as 'a funny little brown dog' ran from the picnic table and plunged into the sea. The otter had sampled most of the food intended for tea, but had finally settled down to eat almost a whole packet of sweet biscuits.

How Fares the Otter?   compiled by B.C.

For more than nine years I have kept a note of the mammals I see each month. Only eleven kinds have been recorded with any frequency; and of these the stoat and weasel score almost entirely from sightings as they ripple across the road in front of my car.

Otter under water by Robert Gillmor

I mention this to emphasise the point that even our commoner predatory mammals are seldom seen alive by those who are out and about a good deal. Foxes and badgers are rather easier because the entrances to their underground homes can be found and patiently watched; but to see an otter is the event of a season, almost of a lifetime. This is partly what makes the protection of mammals such a difficult subject. The rarer breeding birds can be located with certainty and admired from a distance, like the

124

Strathspey ospreys and the snowy owls on Fetlar. But who profits in terms of enjoyment if we protect the otter? So elusive is it that past estimates of status have been largely exercises in conjecture; the most useful data available to the Mammal Society for its recent survey came from the dozen or so packs of otter hounds operating in England, Wales and southern Scotland. The best index is considered to be the number of otters found per hundred days of hunting. Between the beginning of this century and 1937 there was an increase from 64.4 to only 68.1; but a relaxation of pressure of all kinds during the war of 1939-45 led to a substantial rise to 79.8 two years afterwards. Ten years later the index was down to 71.6, but in 1967 it showed a steep decline to 43.6; only 51 otters were despatched by eleven packs, partly due to a deliberate policy of calling hounds off before the kill. Against the general pattern, a 'slight to considerable increase' was reported from the Lake District, the area least affected by contamination from pesticides and, rather surprisingly, by the severe winter of 1962-63. These were temporary factors; increased human pressure on the freshwater resource in the south is likely to continue and intensify. But if the present restraint over pesticides and over the deliberate killing of otters can be maintained, they may be able to adapt themselves to the new situation. The recent appearance of kits in several areas after intervals of years is a hopeful sign.

Otter at Work   by H. G. Woodhead

One day I sat on the rocks at the foot of Armathwaite Weir on the River Eden, watching scores of attempts by salmon of all sizes to jump the falls, and had my reward for remaining practically motionless for an hour and a half. Out of the corner of my eye I saw a small round head appear in the middle of the rapids below the falls. It vanished, then reappeared within a few yards of where I was sitting. An otter was making its way up the side of the river towards the pool below the falls and passed within two yards of my feet. In the pool, which was seething white water, it made a series of head-and-tail dives, like a porpoise. After remaining

125

under water for some considerable time it reappeared with something in its mouth, and swam down the rapids for about a hundred yards, keeping its head above water all the time. As it neared the shallows it rolled over and over as though it had lost control, then made its way to a flat stone standing out of the water. I got my glasses on it and saw it chewing a large eel, head on one side, just like a cat eating fish. It disappeared again, and after some time I saw it advancing once more through the rapids and repeating its manoeuvres, but in the pool it suddenly became aware that it was being watched. It circled the air with its head, faced me for a second motionless, and submerged; that was the last I saw of it. Out of a pool which must have been teeming with fish, the otter had selected an eel, and thus gave support to the widely held view that these animals are actually beneficial in salmon rivers, where eels are known to take a heavy toll of the eggs of the fish.

Otters at Play   by R. M. Lockley

Like dogs and seals, otters have playful habits when young. One October day, on the Welsh coast, I filmed a calf seal leaping at its mother's face, just as a young puppy does; afterwards it tried to climb on her back for a submarine ride. Then in November, perched on a cliff in the Inner Hebrides, I saw the same performance with three otter cubs which were frolicking in the water, their long tails lashing the rough surface of a wind-whipped sea as they repeatedly sprang at and worried the face, head and neck of their dam. The seal's face-worrying cannot have anything to do with food, since the calf is not fed by the cow after suckling is over: in fact, the cow deserts the fat, milk-fed calf after about three weeks of intensive suckling, during which she herself takes no food. But the bitch otter continues to feed her cubs until they are well grown. This was demonstrated when the dam climbed on to the rocks, followed by the three cubs, which were a much greyer brown than the chestnut-coloured mother. The family scrambled over the boulders and presently the dam disappeared, only to come into view again with a spotted plaice in her mouth. One cub leaped at her, snatched the fish and vanished under the boulders with it. She moved over the rough shore, the two remaining cubs still pulling at her great whiskery face and having a joyful rough and tumble with her. Suddenly the bitch seemed to realise that one of her family was missing, because she turned about and began hunting for it, the other two following one on each side of her. At last she discovered the truant under a boulder busily chewing the fish. She grabbed this and began to gallop over the stones and rocks, occasionally stopping for a second or two to crunch the plaice invitingly, so drawing the greedy cubs close on her tail. When they attempted to snatch the fish, she bounded forward with it; being three-quarters her size, they were just that much less agile, and ambled and tumbled behind her with faint whining noises. She reached a shelf low above the water and waited for them to come up with her. Then, diving, splashing and rolling with the cubs in the waves she led them, fish in mouth, across the little bay, until they vanished from sight in the white surf on the rocks of the opposite shore.

Otters' Paradise   by C. G. Chenevix-Trench

In Central India otters abound, and their impudence and contempt for man leave the English observer gasping. They are not hunted and may be studied at close quarters – singly, in parties, or in their annual spring assemblies, which are astonishing spectacles. Under the burning March sun the innumerable meres and irrigation 'tanks' begin to dry up, and later become small, shallow ponds into which the entire fish population is crammed. It is then that the otters gather from far and near to the feast. I once counted over a hundred and fifty of them rioting, gorging and churning to liquid mud an acre or so of turbid fluid. Two of them dragged a five-pound fish to the foreshore at my feet and there, in the attitude of begging dogs, they held the *lanchi* upright on its tail between them and stripped the meat off the backbone from the gills downwards. Then, flinging the half-eaten carcass away, with a squeal they dived in again to renew the massacre. A man was of no more importance to them than a tree-stump.

One sunny but bitterly cold day in February my camp was pitched near a small pond perhaps an acre in extent. A mixed company of pintail and common teal floated asleep on the water. Through the open tent door a brown heap on the opposite shore caught my eye. It flashed in the sun and seemed to move. Soon a head burst through the top of the mound, the jaws gaped in a yawn, and an otter loped into the water, followed by the rest of the heap, ten in all. They mingled with the waterfowl, which showed not the slightest concern, and played among them, mostly floating on their backs all the afternoon. A similar uncanny knowledge of their natural enemies' current mood has been observed in a herd of antelope. A hunted wolf, put up by a pig-sticking party, will run through grazing blackbuck, and not a head be raised.

As a guest of a rajah, I was once housed in his marble pavilion on the embankment of a good-sized lake. One morning the gardener brought me, along with his customary nosegay, a young otter, fat as butter; it lay across his forearms like a pet cat. 'Now,' he said, 'I will show you a *tamasha*. We will put the cub in the water, and then the mother will bite its ear as a punishment for straying from its bed in my cabbage-patch, and take it home again.' Gently we lowered the cub into the water where it paddled in circles, whining pitifully. An otter fishing out in the lake lifted its head and swam straight towards us. I could not be sure that it was her offspring's ear that the mother bit, but she did evoke a sharp yelp of pain. The cub then climbed on her back and lay along it, its forepaws clasping her neck. She dived more than once on her way to the steps leading to the kitchen garden. Later in the day I saw the cub sleeping soundly on a bed of bamboo leaves among the cauliflowers.

In view of their numbers and boldness, it is curious that one rarely hears of otters attacking people. Once, however, as I waded through dense swamp vegetation after snipe, a furious mask was thrust through the screen of reeds in front of me – ears flat, teeth bared and eyes ablaze. Only violent evasive action saved me. A loaded gun was in my hand, but I could never bring myself to kill an otter.

PIGS

The Pig that Made Good   **by Hartley M. Jenkinson**

Herbert's mother, an elderly Large White, had presented my friend's New Zealand farm with more piglets than even she could manage, so I was given one to take home. For most of the thirty miles I had him on my knee, and on arrival I put him to sleep in a corner of the wood-box in the kitchen. This was a mistake, for as he grew we had to build another wood-box outside. After a month he just about ran the farm and the house.

One week-end I was making him a sty outside, and while resting on a log I idly scratched his back with the saw. From that time he assumed that the main purpose of the saw was to scratch his back, and the expression of ecstasy on his face as he stood quivering with one foot off the ground would have done credit to a film star. When one side was done to his satisfaction he would back round for the same on the other. Next to this he most enjoyed going rabbiting with me. More obedient than a dog, he never barked; but I could not train him to retrieve.

In the spring, when we started to get the land in order for the crops, Herbert was in his element. He would follow the tractor for half an hour or so, then find a shady place for a nap. As soon as we stopped for lunch he would wake up and come over for his share, his appetite growing with his size. One day I set off with the mixing-board, which was mounted on skis like a sled, loaded with manure to mix with the swede seed we were planting in the forty-acre. The lane ran down a hill to the railway crossing, then up the other side to the back of the farm. Herbert got the idea that if he climbed on the sled and had a ride he would save himself a lot of effort. This became a habit which was nearly his undoing. As he grew in girth and weight the sled 'drew' on soft ground like a too heavily laden steamer. On one trip the towing gear broke and left the sled, loaded with manure and Herbert, stuck half way across the railway line.

I pulled the tractor well clear and, hearing the express at Warepa, a mile away, I tried to shoo Herbert off the sled. He would not budge, so using the shovel I levered him off and he rolled on to the shovel, breaking the handle. Next I lugged off the 'super' and tried to fix the towing gear while the express came up with screeching whistle and braked to a stop about thirty yards away. Putting a rope round the sled from the tractor I was able to haul it clear, and waved the train on. The driver heaved a lump of coal and shouted 'What about the pig?' There was Herbert, asleep in the middle of the railway line. The fireman, the guard and I between us rolled him out of the way and, much to the diversion of the passengers, he waddled over to the sled, climbed aboard and went to sleep as the train moved off. I was very annoyed with him, but we soon made it up.

Some days later I took his food out to the sty and whistled his dinner call. This was the 'victory' theme from Beethoven's fifth symphony and usually brought him at a rush; but he was in the orchard and I had to repeat the call three times. In his excitement he forgot where the gate was and made a twenty-mile-an-hour dash for his old getaway-hole which I had carefully mended with wire netting. The netting held, but to this day shows the bulge he made in it, just the shape of his face, only longer. We call it Herbert's Mistake.

A buyer from the freezing works called one day to draft some fat lambs, and Herbert, a good mixer, strolled up as usual to meet the visitor.

'What are you going to do with that chap?' the buyer asked.

'Oh, he's a pet. We keep him for company. I got him as a runt, hand fed. We wouldn't send him to the works.'

'I'm not after him for the works. I'll bet he'd clean up the championship at the A. & P. show. Look at those hams, those shoulders, and that back! He's pure bred, and a boar, isn't he?

130

What made you pick him out of the litter anyway?'

'Well, he always kept his tail up. I reckon that's a good sign.'

We entered Herbert for the show and put him through his paces. On the day he could do nothing wrong and the judges awarded him the 'Champion of champions' ticket. His progeny are now scattered all over New Zealand, and he was in his element with plenty of good food, attention, and lady callers at regular intervals. No more manure sleds for him. He rode in a rubber-tyred cushioned float like porcine royalty, and he played the part perfectly.

This Little Pig Stayed at Home   by Alice L. Allen

Cho-cho was a young pig belonging to our nearest neighbours in the bush. They had bought him from a Zulu who explained to them, in his limited English, that the pig was to him 'almost as a brother.' Probably he had been born and brought up in the man's hut, which would explain why he objected so strongly to his sty. He would try to push his way out whenever the gate was opened to feed him, and one winter evening he escaped. We all turned out to help in the search, hunting the bush and calling 'Cho-cho' until we were tired. At last we gave him up for lost, and our neighbours asked us in for coffee before we went home. When we trooped into their dining-room, Cho-cho got up from the fireside there, grunted and wagged his little string tail in welcome.

Desperate Measure   by L. A. N. Downer

I was watching three young pigs at a trough on a friend's farm. Two were feeding, but whenever the third and smallest tried to get near the trough he was relentlessly nipped, jostled and squeezed until forced to retreat. At last, in apparent despair, he gave up and trotted away. Then, at a distance of about twenty yards, he suddenly turned and came hurtling back at full speed, aiming at the backsides of his feasting companions. The impact was such that he not only sent them flying in opposite directions but upset the trough as well. I left him enjoying the fruits of his superior strategy.

131

Can Pigs Swim?   by Eric F. Rochelle

On my Severnside farm I still keep a few sows, more for company than profit; and when necessary I borrow a boar from a neighbour. One cold morning a farmer across the river telephoned to say there was a boar at large on his farm; had I lost one? After driving the five miles round by Bridgnorth – our nearest crossing – I found Charley the boar, wet and covered with mud and looking very sorry for himself. He must have swum the river which at that time was 50 yds. wide and running full spate. Have you heard of any similar incidents?

[The legend that a pig cannot swim without cutting its own throat with its forefeet has been disproved from time to time. In the Winter 1957 issue there was an account of a 10-week-old pig which swam the river Dart at a point where it was 400 yds. wide, and was with difficulty prevented from making the return journey. – *Editors*.]

PINE MARTENS

Pine Martens in Wester Ross   by Sealgair

I have a vivid childhood memory of a picture of a pine marten, described as possessing a throat patch of 'creamy-white sometimes tinged with orange'. So, fifty years later, it was like a dream come true when I suddenly became aware that martens were visiting the house we had built in Wester Ross, on rock thirty feet above the shore of a sea loch. A large slab of Torridonian sandstone to the east makes a natural bird-table. Rocky escarpments, on which oaks maintain a precarious hold, are part of the surrounding hills, which rise to about 800 ft. at the highest visible point.

We put suet out for the tits, suspending it from hooks in the window-shutters, hopefully out of reach of feral cats. This and other scraps for the birds, with plentiful blaeberries and rowans in the garden, may have largely contributed to the arrival of our first pine marten.

132

Pine marten by Diana Brown

The adult, judged by those measured against our window while on the sill outside, varies in length from 2 to 2¾ ft., and stands seven or eight inches high. The colour ranges, between individuals and according to time of year, from chestnut to a warm mole; the muzzle, legs and tail, most bushy in autumn and winter, are a very dark brown. The feet, with light horn-coloured and non-retractable claws, are remarkably large. The ears, permanently erect and seldom (if ever) twitched, are rounded and limned with short honey-beige hair. The nose is brown, and the throat patch indeed varies from creamy-white to apricot. We distinguish individuals by the pattern of dark on it. The sexes are not easily told apart, but the male appears to be more heavily built and has a wider skull. Martens make great use of their sense of smell; their hearing is acute, but I believe that they are long-sighted and have some difficulty in focusing near-by objects.

The feet of young martens appear much too large for their bodies, their coats have a softer look, and their tails are rather thin when we first see them abroad with their mother. This is usually towards the end of June or early July, as they are born in late April. By November they are almost as large as their parents but appear less mature.

During the past few years scarcely a day has passed without a visit from martens, though the timing varies greatly. In high summer we may see a mother with three young playing together over the feed rock, as we did last year. She remained on guard, but the young scampered here and there, tumbling each other over by placing a small brown nose under a flank, watching while their mother secured a piece of cheese from a shutter-hook, then chasing her like a pack of long-tailed bear cubs and disappearing into the heather. We have also seen them balancing along the top of a wattle fence or being led in single file up the trunk of an ancient oak which grows out over the shore at an angle of 45° and was presumably selected as an easy climb. Otherwise we seldom see one in a tree; even when alarmed they are inclined to run rather than to climb, though there are trees close by. One winter, during the first snows, a young marten came with its mother and gave a most enchanting performance, playing like a kitten, rolling, stretching, bouncing stiff-legged and picking up snow in its mouth. Then, springing into a clump of heather, it lay down, head just over the top, before rushing out at its mother.

Martens have fed inside our bedroom for some years now, from a tray placed on the window-sill close by my head. It contains chopped cheese and raspberry jam, and has often been refilled four or five times in a night. The martens will feed even when the room is lit and we are drinking tea or listening to the first news bulletin. My greatest triumph occurred recently when one fed on the sill a few feet from me while I was undressing; even the placing of my clothes on a chair just behind him did not affect his composure. Occasionally a foot slips and a marten lands on the bed, only to spring back on to the sill. Once or twice the visitor has explored the house first, eventually going out as he came in, but aided now by the lights and a convenient chair. The overhang of the sill and its slippery painted surface make difficult a leap direct from the floor four feet below.

We often include a pullet's egg in the diet; and it is fascinating to watch a marten take one from the sill. It picks up the egg firmly, holds it transversely between its jaws and lowers its body carefully over the edge while its hind feet, twisted in remarkable fashion, enable it to retain a grip on the sill. This flexibility and the fur between the pads appear to assist martens greatly when climbing or taking a tree-bait tied to a thin branch.

Our experience does not bear out the statement that in an encounter with a wild cat a pine marten would prove superior. If there is a cat in the garden, we see no martens. When one appears suddenly while a marten is feeding on the sill, the marten is on top of the shutter in a twinkling and remains there until the cat moves or is driven off.

The call of the young marten is aptly likened to 'the sound of tearing cloth'. There are other calls: huffy warning growls by adults and a sort of continuous whicker which we have heard from two martens feeding in our room at either end of the tray.

Although we are specially favoured by the presence of pine martens in our garden and house, anyone living within their range could achieve similar success by attracting them with suitable food; and in our experience the marten is certainly not the ferocious animal it is often made out to be.

POSSUMS

Tightrope Act   by A. Len Moore

A half-grown grey brush-tailed possum living in my eucalyptus is a capable walker along the high wire. At dusk it comes down, crosses a path and climbs 20 ft. up a pole to a crossbar. Only its dusty yellow belly discloses its movements as it steadies itself and sets out along the power line, faster than a man can walk. I have seen it falter only once: it paused, clung on with all claws, balanced again and continued – almost unchecked, its brush held straight out behind like a rudder. The possum makes no other use of its tail, though the tip is prehensile. There are several rewards for this junior Blondin. On its way to my neighbour's roof it is well clear of traffic and safe from cats and dogs. At journey's end ripe pine nuts hang over the slates – one jump to an undisturbed meal.

PYGMY GLIDERS

Pygmy Glider   by M. Mommaerts

After a period of bad bush fires we were walking in the Blue Mountains when we saw a pygmy or feather-tailed glider hopping over a burnt-out area like a kangaroo. Few Australians have seen this tiny marsupial with a body of only 2 to 3 in., though its feather-like tail is as long again. This has been evolved for gliding, but can also be used to grip; the flying membrane extends from wrist to ankle. The female builds a fairly substantial nest of gum leaves and bark in a hole 50 ft. above ground and produces a litter of three or four; she has only four teats and her pouch cannot hold more. The young may remain with their parents, and groups of up to 16 are on record. Their age in the wild is not known, but a male in the London Zoo lived nearly four years. The pygmy glider is protected in Australia so, after photographing it on my hand, we put it into a small tree and watched it glide from branch to branch.

PYGMY SHREWS

The Pygmies are Friendly   by Joyce Averil Burgess

The pygmy shrew who treats my kitchen as if it were his own (his sex is pure conjecture) enters by squeezing under the door and also uses a mouse-hole under a cupboard. Food fills his thoughts, and he takes it fearlessly from my hand. Sometimes I hear his faint whispering whistle when he discovers something of interest. He loves to explore, climbing on to my shoe and then up stockings or slacks without hesitation. His feet are so light that often I do not know he is there; once he arrived on my arm and was almost into my soup before my exclamation of surprise caused him to slip swiftly to the ground. Frequently when he is near me he sits up straight, wuffling his nose and whiskers and waving his paws, plainly asking for the crumbs he is sure to get. He never refuses what I offer but, if he does not like it, carries it off to some safe place, as I discovered when putting on a shoe that was full of cheese crumbs and toast. Once – I do not know how – he fell into a jam-jar, but I found him before it was too late. He rummaged inside a bag of garden lime and was covered in fine dust. As he ran off, I wondered how he was going to get clean and whether the lime would harm his eyes or even kill him if he tried to wash it off. A few minutes later he was scampering over the floor, not a sign of dust on his dark coat. One shake must have cleared the sleek velvet, and once more the business of food-hunting was in full swing. He is clever at balancing on the slippery edge of a saucer to sip the milk, of which he is so fond. It seems to tickle his whiskers, because he shakes it off in a cloud of spray and goes all skittery in the middle of the saucer, dabbling his paws at speed and flipperting his nose in and out. Then he rushes round the kitchen and is back

137

again before I have time to see where he has gone, to repeat it all or leap into the milk with a delightful plop. If he meets a common shrew quietly sipping the milk, there is a great game for a few seconds until they disappear in different directions, scattering milk everywhere and leaving a dainty pattern of little footmarks round the saucer.

RABBITS

Buster   by G. E. Wells

My seal-pointed Siamese cat, Cleo, brought it home, an anonymous rag of soaking wet fur which she dumped on the kitchen floor. There it lay limp and, as I thought, dead. Cleo mouthed it over, making her deep throaty growls which mean 'Come and look!' My blue-pointed Siamese, known as Mum, obligingly went over, but I continued with what I was doing. If it had been Mum calling, I would have gone at once, for she was my collecting cat. For years she had been bringing me wild creatures, from mice and birds to moths and snakes, all completely unharmed. Cleo's catches, nearly all maimed or dead, were strictly for eating; but this time her talking was not followed by the usual gruesome noises. In fact I detected a purr. When I did go to look, she was licking a baby rabbit and cuddling it. The odd growl was for Mum to keep her distance.

I judged the tiny creature to be about three weeks old. When it tried to stagger off to a dark corner, Cleo prevented it with velvet paw but somewhat boisterously. So I warmed up an empty goldfish bowl and fitted corrugated cardboard in the bottom, with a little hay on top. I let the cats sit over this, watching the rabbit within. At intervals I fed it a dandelion leaf dipped in milk. The first, which I had to push gently into its mouth with a match-stick, was pushed out again; and the creature tried to hide under the hay. I tried again with the tip of the leaf and gave the cats some meat to eat outside the bowl. This time the rabbit gave a couple of chews and eventually ate the leaf to the end, and then another.

page 139
An Atlantic seal pup, photographed on the Farne Islands

The orphan

It is a mistake to give a baby rabbit quiet and a box in which to hide, with food available, under the impression that at dusk it will come out and feed. Usually it tries only to escape, and then nearly always dies. At this age animals need fussing and companionship as well as food and warmth. So in default of its mother I had to provide in my kitchen a time-table for survival.

On the second day I named the rabbit Buster, presuming his sex. He lived in his glass home in the glare of publicity for a week, seeing and being seen all the hours of daylight. Whenever convenient I put him out on the floor with the cats for exercise, after making sure that Cleo still regarded him as her adopted waif and not as her next dinner. They rode herd on him like a couple of zealous sheepdogs with a wayward lamb, and seemingly taught him that substitute kittens do not run and hide in the face of danger and strangers. A visitor who tickled him under the chin retreated with a ruffled 'Goddarn it, it's bitten me!' Buster was inclined to nip any stranger who took liberties after that.

His diet enlarged from dandelions and milk to all suitable garden herbage and titbits from the kitchen; his favourites were digestive biscuits and bananas. He grew apace, and the second week I transferred him to a large plastic bowl with a sheet of mesh over the top. I removed this in the morning to feed him, after which he often took a prodigious leap up at my shoulder. He liked to sit there as the cats did, preferring it to being held or restrained. As he gave no sign of his intention, I often failed to provide a helping hand and, with no hooks to his claws, he came some ignominious croppers.

When Buster was six weeks old, I put him outdoors in a wire mink-cage with a box of hay inside, close to the door where he could have our company. I still brought him in to play with the cats, or let him free outside when it was fine. In the early days he was easily induced with a biscuit to return to his cage. Cleo spent a lot of time with him, either sitting and watching, or doing her sheepdog act if he was free. When a wandering dog appeared on the scene, Cleo promptly attacked it; but in the shemozzle Buster was panicked out of known territory to a thicket in the field. Although I intended to free him eventually, I did not think he would yet survive attacks by foxes, cats and dogs for a day; so I wasted the afternoon enticing him back to the fold with the cats' help.

After this I made him a little elastic collar and attached a piece of string, to hold or trail. My purpose was not to teach him to lead like a dog, but to have a method of retrieving him and a remote control over what he ate. He seemed to be attracted to the more poisonous plants, and with a little tug I could stop him in mid bite. He hated it and bit through the string in two ticks, so I had to change the first two feet to light flex. His mother must have told him about snares. Soon his confidence in me returned, and he took little notice of the lead. But I now had to follow him at a distance of about twelve feet, instead of letting him out and collecting him up after a suitable spell of freedom.

As he grew older and ventured farther from home, the caution and wariness of the wild creature came swimming to the surface. On being let out he would instantly sit up to look round and make sure that all was as usual and safe. Then he would go through his endearing little routine of hops and skips of joy that had started in his kitchen days. Once on fresh ground he intensified his reconnoitring. He appeared most annoyed that he could not shoot up trees like the cats and, when following the hedgerow, scrambled on to stumps whenever possible.

Although Buster's acquired tricks often made me laugh, I was more interested in his natural traits and potential for looking after himself in the wild. When we came to a rough patch, he measured out his hops towards home, going back and forth many times. He bit off weed stems and brambles and pushed them to the side with his forepaws; and he tested the way back before making a further advance. Now I knew that rabbit runs through thick scrub and grass were really worked at. He also began to stamp his hind foot when he thought danger was near.

I added another mink-cage to the first and gave Buster a fair amount of hay, grass and leaves. Completely camouflaging himself with them, he made a seat where he stayed, quiet and still as any wild rabbit, from after breakfast until tea-time, coming out only to hob-nob with Cleo or to take a special titbit from me. He had always done a lot of grooming and washing of his coat; now his toilet was meticulous, to remove any give-away scents before he retired for the day.

Buster would soon be five months old, and a wild creature should go free. Deciding that it would be best to release him in surroundings he knew, I took him to the nearest rabbit warren and made him familiar with the land between. He showed neither interest in the burrows nor the slightest inclination to dig. I introduced him to a hollow tree and near at hand made another refuge under an old chicken ark in the field. I let Deb, my dalmatian, chase him a little and, as he was exceedingly spry and agile when he did not wish to be caught, I reckoned he had a fair chance. But there were foxes, stoats and weasels; he might well regard strange cats and dogs as friends or at least as harmless; and there were boys with guns and poachers with ferrets and nets if he took to underground life – a hundred dangers against which I could not warn him.

On a fine warm day, at tea-time when he was used to going free and was at his most alert, I finally let him out. I left the front and back entrances to his cage partly open in the hope that he would have the sense to go right through if chased by stoat or weasel, and to stop in the middle if it was a dog, fox or large cat. About eleven o'clock I had a look round with a torch. Buster was sitting three feet up on a stump in the garden hedge where Cleo often sat. It looked a silly place for an intelligent rabbit to spend a draughty night; but I went to bed and hoped for the best.

Early next morning there was no sign of him. After breakfast I wandered in vain where I thought he was most likely to be. I took the dogs out for their walk and, coming back by the road, found Buster sitting on top of a bank, suicidally exposed. I shooed him down across the pasture to the hedge nearer home. He looked a bit bewildered and bedraggled from the dew. I gave

143

him the biscuit and banana I had brought and left him. At midday he was sitting in the open but had tried to pull grass up around him, and kept his ears flattened when we went past. I told him that was 'good', without otherwise disturbing him.

It rained almost continuously that night; but by morning the gale had blown itself out and the sun was shining as I set out for my early walk with the dogs. Buster was hopping about skittishly under the trees on the road side of the field. He looked dry, spruce and pleased with himself. I gave him his titbits and, when children on ponies came clattering by, he nonchalantly hopped off across the field to disappear under the ark. This was fine; it was just about the safest refuge, and he was more independent than when using the mink-cages as home. I saw him nearly every day to give him biscuits and other delicacies, and on warm sunny days I often spotted him in his seat. After the first week or so this was not easy, as he converted the spot into a camouflaged hide. But I was bothered that he had taken the roadside hedge as his main playground, probably because he could follow it back to the garden.

After a few days I stopped leaving food in his old haunts or doing anything to encourage him there. I considered whether I should not feed him at all and ignore him if we met; but to disappoint him when he hopped out of the hedge to greet us was too much. In fact, as the days went safely by, I grew careless. One early morning Buster was sitting up in the road taking his biscuit from my hand, with the dogs watching, when an old man came silently round the corner on a bicycle. He glided by as Buster made off and, craning his head round, no doubt to see if the apparition was true, wobbled off the road into the ditch.

Buster now seemed completely in command of his free life. One day he turned up with a bitten and bloody ear, but his confidence was in no way diminished. By the end of his fourth month of freedom I had ceased to worry about his life of hazard, so it was all the more of a shock one morning to find his body, with the bitten ear scars, by the gate at the end of the drive. There was no mark or sign of violence on it, and his end remains a mystery. I felt sad, for, in a much less spectacular way, I had enjoyed an experience as rewarding as Joy Adamson's with Elsa the lioness.

ONE early July day, in Oxfordshire, we had to slow down the car to avoid running over a weasel pursued from one side of the road to the other by a rabbit. The weasel several times tried to get back but was always headed off by fierce rushes from the rabbit, which finally returned to its own side of the road, seemingly victorious. I noticed that the rabbit carried its ears erect. *S.S.*

ONLOOKER to man digging furiously at rabbit burrow: 'How d'you know there's a rabbit in that hole?' 'I seen 'im come out.'

RATS

A Near Disaster by I. M. Watson

Our dogs had found a rat-hole under the gnarled roots of a giant Scots pine, which spread over the top of a bank and ran beneath a hawthorn. All day, at intervals, they had been on the bank trying to get at the nest. Then, towards sundown, I saw the mother rat come out with a baby in her mouth; evidently she had decided to find new quarters. Already a thin film of ice covered the water in the bird bath on the lawn, and the twigs of the hawthorn sparkled with hoar frost. The old rat stood still, her head raised anxiously, and sniffed the air; along the bank behind her ran six or seven more young rats. She raised herself on her hind legs and, still holding the baby, ran lightly along the larger branches of the hawthorn until she reached the middle of it, where it grew into a thicket. Then she turned and went down on the other side, carefully making her way between the branches, but the baby rat became caught between some thorny twigs. The mother stopped and tried to extricate it, pulling it gently this way and that, but without success. She stood on her hind legs and tried frantically with her front paws to get the little creature out. Suddenly there was a movement at the root of the pine and, like a streak of lightning, another large rat dashed up the thorntree and on to the opposite branch. There followed one of the most remarkable displays of sagacity and determination I have ever seen, as the two old rats worked together, one carefully pushing and the other gently pulling, to free the baby. The frosty twigs shone and swayed as they slipped and turned, tugged and pushed, their bodies silhouetted against the crimson sunset. Finally the male rat bit the twigs and tore them away from the small body with his teeth, until at last it dangled free. Then he turned and ran away quickly, and the mother, again carrying the baby in her mouth, sped down the bush in the opposite direction.

SEALS

Battle Royal   by Anne Quekett

As I sat on a rocky platform on the eastern side of Rathlin Island, some four miles off the north Antrim coast, I was startled to hear heavy breathing almost at my feet and saw that a big grey bull seal had come close inshore to inspect me. After some minutes he disappeared and I was looking for his partner, as seals are not often seen singly, when there was a sudden turmoil just off the rocks. The bull rose grunting and wheezing in his effort to maintain his grip on a giant conger-eel, which he held near the tail. The great length of the eel's body arched high out of the water and then flattened along the surface. While the seal tried to take a surer grip near the head, the conger reared its gleaming coils up and above the seal's head, striking at the jaws and finally twisting in a strangle-hold about the thick bull-neck. Time after time the pair submerged and rose struggling together, until the eel released its grip momentarily and was seized beneath the head and bitten deep in the belly, so that the water was crimson about them. The seal now began to show signs of distress. He seemed to rest briefly, unable to do more than keep his hold on the eel, which was still fighting gamely, the slap of its tail sounding on the water and on its adversary's body. The end of the struggle was a breath-taking spectacle. The seal dipped his great head and, gripping the conger below the water with his flippers, raised himself slowly, drawing back his head; steadily he tore a long strip of living flesh from head to tail and devoured it. The sounds of tearing flesh and crunching jaws came sharply across to me on that still afternoon, until there remained only the tail and bared vertebrae, still lashing for release, though feebly now. Then these, too, were eaten to the last mouthful. Tired and replete, the seal heaved his great shining body on to the rock platform where, unconcerned at my presence, he lay basking in the last warmth of the sun. The whole struggle had occupied fully ten minutes.

Playing Ball   by M. Traill-Clouston

Off North Ronaldsay to the north of Orkney lies a skerry, home of a colony of grey seals. While I was watching them one day, a crofter-fisherman friend told me that they did a great deal of damage to lobster pots. When leaping and playing, they became entangled with the ropes, twisting and shortening them so much that the floats were held under at high water and could not be located. I felt this was rather a tall story until, some months later, I was on Glimpsholm at the eastern end of Scapa Flow. Bobbing on the pale blue winter sea was a large fluorescent orange float, marking a lobster pot and making a brilliant splash of colour in the sunshine. The head of a large seal appeared near the float and the animal proceeded to cruise round it, dive close to it and push it with its nose, twisting this way and that and finally disappearing, as did the float. I watched for some time, and again on my way home, but the float did not reappear.

SHEEP

Milking Sheep   by J. P. Maule

Most people think of sheep as producers of meat and wool, but in parts of southern Europe and in the eastern Mediterranean they are kept primarily for their milk. The fat-tailed breed found in Turkey, Syria, Palestine and Cyprus is very hardy and particularly

147

suited to the poor conditions and extremes of heat and cold which occur in these countries. As their name implies, these sheep have characteristic broad tails in which they store up reserves of fat for use in times of scarcity. The wool is long and coarse, and is used mostly for carpets, although the peasants make themselves clothes from it.

Sheep's milk, often mixed with goat's milk, is the main source of cheese, yaourt and other local milk products in the Near East. It contains from six to ten per cent. of butterfat compared with about four per cent. for cow's milk. A ewe yields on the average about a pint a day, but some give two, and in Palestine selected ewes on Jewish farms give four or five pints. These high-yielding ewes are the result of many years' selection of the best animals for breeding, as well as of exceptionally good feeding. Few of the peasant farmers feed their flocks specially for milk production, and the sheep graze on fallow land or on common grazing or uncultivated land. Only at lambing time are they fed with grain or grazed on green forage crops. During the hot, dry summer they are run over stubbles and fallows where their diet consists mainly of the leaves and stalks of cereals and grasses. It is then that they have to rely to some extent on their reserves of fat.

Mutton or lamb is the favourite meat of most of the peoples of the Near East. The Arabs invariably have whole sheep, stuffed with all manner of delicacies, roasted on special occasions, and the young, tender lamb – usually killed when only a few weeks old so that the ewe can be milked – is the main source of meat for the Cypriots.

The Twin   by Leslie Halward

In a corner of the orchard, away from the others, a ewe is standing with her new-born lamb. All the morning a still, thick fog has hidden and chilled the countryside. Now the warm sun is shining, drying the lamb and giving him strength. He feels the gentle heat of it on his back as, with legs trembling and tail quivering, he nuzzles and bunts at the matted wool under his mother's belly.

Unable to find the teat, he bunts and nuzzles harder, complaining in a thin and muted bleat. The ewe, impatient, moves suddenly, and the lamb staggers and falls to his knees, his hind legs spread and bent, his head back and his dry, searching mouth still open. Slowly his head falls forward, and he remains like that for several seconds, too weak to raise himself.

The ewe is restless, unable to give all her attention to her lamb. Ignoring him, she walks a few steps in a half-circle, grunting a little and moving her head and shoulders from side to side, as if burrowing her way through a hedge. Suddenly she lies down, with her fore legs stretched out straight, her big sides heaving rhythmically and her breath coming like puffs of steam from her distended nostrils. After a few moments she shakes her head again and heaves herself to her feet. She walks to the lamb and begins to lick his face, baaing repeatedly, reassuring him. At the sound and touch of her, the lamb struggles up, and the ewe manoeuvres herself so that he finds the teat easily. He sucks noisily, trembling with delight.

But again the ewe moves away, leaving the lamb unsatisfied and bewildered, swaying slightly on his unsteady legs as he turns to follow her with his eyes. The ewe walks a few paces slowly, her head hanging; and watching her, the lamb springs into the air almost a foot. His legs collapse as he hits the ground and he falls on to his side with a soft thud, all the breath knocked out of him. The ewe hears his thin cry, but she does not go to him or even turn her head. With a low grunt, she herself sinks to the grass again. Digging her fore feet into the turf, she strains, throwing back her head. The lamb rises cautiously and with prodding feet goes up to her. When he reaches her, the ewe stops straining and half rises. The lamb is at her back now, nuzzling frantically. He drops to his knees and buries his sharp black face in her wool. With a quick movement she pushes him over, so that he falls close to her. Then gently she lowers herself on to him, her soft body holding his legs so that he is unable to get up. The lamb wriggles and two or three times tries to free his legs. Then he lies still.

149

When the lamb is still, the ewe once more settles herself. She digs her fore feet into the turf so that she is in a half-sitting position. She stretches her neck, so that her nose is pointing to the sky. The heaving rhythm of her body starts and her breath comes and goes in great gasps. With each strain her hind quarters rise slightly from the ground. Except for her laboured breathing, the ewe is silent. The lamb at her back lies motionless, overcome by the warmth of her body, almost asleep.

Within two minutes the head and shoulders of another lamb have appeared, and half-way through the birth, in pain and impatience, the ewe stands up, the fore quarters of the living lamb protruding from her, wet and steaming. The ewe baas once and turns first one way and then the other spasmodically, trying to look behind her. Then, with a shuddering sigh, she drops quickly to the ground. Stamping with her fore feet, half standing, her breath rattling through her gaping mouth, she pushes the lamb out and sinks full length, utterly exhausted. Her first lamb, freed, bleating joyfully, begins to push his face into her back, again searching.

The second lamb, his thin sides rising and falling rapidly, moves his head and then his legs and utters his first faint cry; and the ewe, with a sudden determined movement, gets to her feet and begins licking him. The first lamb, delirious with joy, has found a teat and is sucking ravenously, and the ewe, while attending to the second one, helps the first by moving her body and legs to make it easier for him. She cleans the second lamb and the sun warms him, and soon he begins to push his front feet into the earth and then to lift his slender hind quarters, trembling. Time after time he tries to stand up, as his mother licks him and baas almost without pausing, encouraging him; and at last his body is precariously supported. Using his legs for the first time, he moves to where the other lamb, his brother, is gulping greedily.

Ten minutes later, their strength used up, momentarily satisfied, the lambs lie on either side of the ewe, their eyes closed, resting. The ewe is not resting. She is moving from one to the other, licking the closed eyes and the pointed ears and the tight-curled wool, going back and forth, baaing and murmuring quite contentedly.

Shetland Sheep   by Richard Perry

Though no beauty, the Shetland sheep is an interesting animal, with a history. Up to the end of the bronze age its ancestor, the little Turbary, or peat-sheep, was the only domestic breed in Europe. Despite the fact that it stood only twenty-two inches at the shoulder, and that its fleece weighed less than one pound, the Turbary was the backbone of the Scottish woollen industry from neolithic times to the Middle Ages. Today, the breed most closely resembling it is the moorit-brown (fawn-coloured) Soay sheep introduced to St. Kilda by the Norsemen several hundred years ago. The Shetland might be termed an improved 'modern' type of Soay; though numbers of them still retain the moorit-coloured fleece (the lambs being born nigger-brown like Soay lambs), the majority are now white, as were their close relatives, the pink-nosed, fine-woolled *Seana chaorich bheaga*, the little old sheep of the Gaels. These were the only sheep in the Scottish Highlands until the middle of the eighteenth century, when farmers from the southern uplands began pushing north into the Highlands with their Black-face, and subsequently Cheviot, sheep. The clearances of the old Highland townships quickly resulted in the total expulsion of the little old sheep from all parts of Britain except the Shetlands, which have also been invaded by the Black-face and Cheviot breeds, together with a few Swaledales and the ubiquitous Border Leicester ram.

There are probably no pure-bred Shetland sheep in existence, but the breed is a dominant one and, though there has been much crossing with Cheviots, the moorit retains its breed characteristics – the small, lean, angular body, with what little fat there is on the rump, and the long 'dished' face and flared nostrils; the fine silky wool; and the ability to survive for half the year on a diet of mosses and seaweed, and yet rear one, or two, good lambs in the spring.

151

And no matter whether all the ewes and rams in a flock be white or not, each spring brings its quota of hardy, coloured lambs – some chocolate-brown moorit, some black, some 'catmuggit' or parti-coloured. There is also an occasional grey lamb, like a tabby cat, from those grizzled ewes known as sheilas, every hair of whose black wool is tipped with white.

We do not know whether there were white sheep among those moorits introduced into Shetland by the Vikings, but it is significant that moorit sheep taken to the Scottish mainland begin to lose their colour very shortly after arrival. Furthermore, there are two types of sheep ground in Shetland: the heather or black ground, and the grassy holms or islands. Remove your moorits from black to green ground and in no more than three years they, too, lose their colour. Similarly, put your flock on to green ground and the fine lustrous wool begins to coarsen. It is always the crofter's score or two of starvelings, grazing round the year on the poor grasses, mosses and stunted heather of the semi-deserted townships and on the 'scattald' – that part of the hill reserved for the crofters' communal grazing – that bear the finest-textured wool. As the wool of Cheviots pastured in Shetland is also of a finer texture than that of those on the mainland of Scotland, you can draw your own conclusions as to whether it is the poor quality of the Shetland herbage or some mineral deficiency in the soil that produces these phenomena.

At the beginning of the last century there were only about 30,000 sheep in Shetland. Today, there are more than five times this number, despite the loss of 50,000 during an almost unprecedentedly hard winter recently. But to be strictly accurate, more sheep died of a stomach complaint in the spring than of actual starvation during the freeze-up. So long as a moorit can have access to the tangle on the sea-shore it can find sufficient nourishment to keep going. This population works out at about one sheep to three acres of land or twelve per head of the human population outside Lerwick, the islands' port and capital wherein six of the twenty thousand inhabitants are concentrated.

A few farmers in Shetland work exclusively with the Shetland breed, but the bulk of these sheep are owned by the crofters – for the very good reason that the wool provides the raw material for the Shetland hosiery. This cottage industry, turning out Fair Isle jumpers, berets, gloves and other knitted articles by the thousand, now brings into Shetland an annual income actually exceeding that of the herring and white fisheries combined, and, for the first time in Shetland's history, makes the crofter more or less independent of the ups and downs of fishing. So this little animal, primitive though it is by ordinary sheep-farming standards, is very nearly worth its weight in gold to the Shetland crofter. During the winter he, or more usually his wife or daughter, ekes out the starvation rations of his dozen or score of sheep with cabbages, potatoes and crusts of bread, and perhaps a little grain and oil-nuts; and by the end of the winter it is difficult to keep them out of the living-room. Though most of the crofters keep their own rams, these fine fellows with their curling horns – the ewes have only rudimentary horns or none at all – are usually sold at the end of their season, as they tend to grow too strong and wild to submit to tethering. With the approach of the lambing season at the end of April, the crofters tether out their ewes in pairs on the crofting: just as the crofter's cow, after being stalled in the byre night and day for more than half the year, is also tethered out in May or June, and will never be off the tether until she goes indoors again at the back-end of the year. Grazing is too scanty in Shetland for stock to run free anywhere except on the scattald.

Like all primitive sheep, the Shetland breed, expecially the coloured ewes, are excellent milkers, and one in every five or six will successfully rear twin lambs, long-legged little creatures, no bigger in body than a cat, which thrive and mature more quickly than the cross-lambs. Until the lambs can graze, the ewes are kept tethered; then they are allowed to go out to the scattald. While most of the crofters keep a collie or two – not of course the Shetland collie, which is only a toy dog – few of these are even half-trained; so that, when the time comes to 'roo' the sheep late in June or

153

July, there are high jinks on the scattald, as each crofter and his wife, with their companions, chase miles over the hill, endeavouring to cut out and round up their own sheep – distinguished by coloured wools in their ears – from among the couple of hundred belonging to the township.

Though not the barbarous practice it is sometimes supposed to be, rooing, or plucking, the wool off the sheep certainly leaves them very bare – much barer than the hand-shears, which the farmers use for their flocks. However, the sheep are not rooed until there is a natural rise in the wool, pushed up by the new hair growing beneath. (In the peat-sheep, incidentally, the wool was underneath the hair.) The fleece averages out at only one and a half pounds in weight, compared to the four or five pounds of the Black-face, or the eight or ten pounds of the Cheviot. This is all that is left of the fleeces on the ewes' backs by this season, for the animals are usually in such poor condition after the long hard winter that a quarter or half of each fleece has long since been left on wire fences and stone dykes. The crofter's wife dispatches her wool crop to the Scottish mills to be carded and spun, for she no longer performs these operations in her own home, and a spinning-mill is only now being erected, over-late, in Shetland. She receives back half the weight of the crop for her own use, and the knitting of it keeps her busy during the long winter evenings.

Shetland Sheep   by John Copland

I cannot agree with Richard Perry that 'rooing', or plucking, the wool from sheep leaves them barer than hand shearing. The reverse is true, because rooing leaves the new fleece intact, whereas shearing removes 25 to 75 per cent of it, and sometimes more. When the new and old fleeces are matted together, rooing is very slow and is tough going for both man and beast, but it leaves the sheep far better protected against a sudden weather change. Richard Perry also puts the proportion of twin lambs far too high; we had one pair of twins out of 200 Shetland ewes and any number above three would have been unusual. Most of the lambs are marked with coloured wools in the ears (when they can be caught), but in the summer or autumn of their first year they are usually marked permanently with variously shaped cuts from the ears. This practice is long established and widespread over the islands. Hand feeding is rare, except after lengthy periods of snow.

[Richard Perry, in his reply, points out that conditions vary from one district to another. It should have been made clear, perhaps, that it was on Bressay that he spent much of his time. On rooing he writes: 'I have both clipped and rooed Shetland sheep, and observed the latter practice, and noted that the rooed sheep were much barer; but, in either case, much depends on the condition of the sheep at shearing time'.]

Unravelling the Evidence   **by Michael L. Ryder**
When bronze-age cloth was first found many years ago, it was thought to have been made from a mixture of sheep's wool and deer hair. The best-known specimens I have examined came from the water-logged oak coffin burials in Denmark about 1200 B.C. The wool had the same brown colour as the fleeces of the feral Soay sheep of Scotland; and my measurements of fibre diameter under the microscope indicated a fleece of similar composition, with the same range of kempy and woolly types. The 'deer hairs' were without doubt the bristly kemp fibres that form the outer coat of primitive sheep. The fact that one sample had an unusually high proportion of wool fibres worried me until I visited St. Kilda to study the moult of the Soay. There I discovered that the fine wool and some of the kemp are shed in spring, but much of the kemp is retained until later in the season. So if the wool, harvested by plucking the loose fibres, were gathered early in the year, the retention of kemps in the skin would mean that fewer would find their way into yarn.

Much wool from the succeeding iron age lacks natural pigment, and a piece of sheepskin from the salt workings at Hallstatt in Austria, dated about 500 B.C., had white kemp and wool still attached. In a Scythian skin of 400 B.C. from Central Asia the kemps had been replaced by less coarse hairs.

Some dyed wool from the Cave of the Letters near the Dead Sea, dated second century A.D., was the most rewarding ancient material I have studied: it made the findings from all other specimens fall into place in an evolutionary sequence. Professor Yadin of Israel sent it to me when I was lecturing in Australia. The wool appeared fine to the naked eye and seemed to support historical records by classical writers; but when I was able to examine it under the microscope, I was excited to find that it contained the same proportion of medium fibres as most of the Dead Sea Scrolls. Was the 'fine wool' of the ancients not a true fine wool? Could this be the evolutionary link between the oldest and most primitive hairy types and the modern improved fleeces?

This midway fleece could have arisen if the hairy outer fibres had narrowed to produce medium fibres. Had these thinned further to fine, the fleece would have become the homogeneous true fine wool. A few true fine wools among the parchments of the Dead Sea Scrolls showed that this change had already taken place. But if from this midway fleece the medium fibres had remained unaltered and the fine fibres had coarsened, a true medium fleece would have resulted, similar to the modern long wool.

Roman textiles from Northern Europe, in a whole range of types, showed these evolutionary changes. There were coloured wools, presumably from native sheep, of both kempy and woolly midway types like the Soay, as well as true fine and true medium wools. Unfortunately it is not always certain whether Roman cloth found in Britain was imported or manufactured locally. Some cloth from Newstead, a fort on the Scottish Borders, had naturally pigmented wool, suggesting native sheep; one yarn was kempy and the other of true medium type. One yarn from the Falkirk 'tartan' was kempy and pigmented, and the other was fine and white. The pigmented Huntcliffe cloth from a watch-tower on the Yorkshire coast had a generalised medium yarn and a fine yarn.

The Romans may well have introduced the first improved

page 157
The first of a pair of twin lambs, immediately after birth

page 158
(above) *The second twin lamb is born;* (below) *first faltering steps*

Soay   Romney Marsh

white sheep into Britain. Most medieval illustrations show white-faced polled animals which may be fairly directly descended from the Roman sheep. The modern Ryeland breed is perhaps a survivor and the Romney may trace his ancestry by way of the medieval Longwool to the Roman imports. In the more northerly and westerly parts of Britain, where the influence of the Romans was less strong, their white sheep and the brown native Soay may have produced crosses that later emerged as breeds: the Welsh Mountain and the Cheviot of the Scottish Border.

Parts of the extreme north, including the Northern and Western Isles of Scotland, were occupied by Norse settlers from about A.D. 800-1400 and remains of Norse cloth from these parts contain more kempy wool than either Roman or medieval cloth from farther south. Some of the native sheep remaining in Orkney have kempy fleeces; others have woolly ones, and it is from these, by selection, that the modern Shetland derives. The Vikings who came from Denmark to occupy eastern and northern England may have introduced the hairy black-faced horned stock, the forbears of the Swaledale and Scottish Blackface. Similar sheep remain on

Welsh Mountain   Scottish Blackface

the Continent; and their origins appear to lie in Asia, taking us
back to the Scythian skin of 400 B.C. – but I am still seeking textile
or parchment evidence for this.   *Drawings by R. Wise*

NORFOLK farmer: 'Sheep don't want to hear the church bells
ring in the same pasture twice — can't abide the taste of their own
smell.'

The Lost Sheep   by P. F. Downes

Some years ago, while working on a country road, I heard a ewe
calling from the other side of the hedge. Although she did not
sound really distressed, there was a note of urgency and inquiry in
her voice. Very conveniently, there was a ladder against a pole
near by, and I climbed it to look over the hedge. There she was,
close behind it, still calling and listening. The rest of the flock were
some distance away, but presently one of them lifted her head,
looked in the direction of the call and answered. Then she walked
slowly towards the road, answering each bleat as she came, until at
last the anxious one heard her. The pleased note sounding in her
next call was unmistakably, as she walked to join the friend who

had come to her aid. Being completely blind, when she could no longer hear the others she was lost indeed.

Battering Ram   by Richard Clough

An old Westmorland farmhouse was recently extended by the addition of a lounge with a picture window. Scarcely had the workmen finished when down the fellside wandered an old Herdwick ram. Its attention was caught by the glittering expanse of glass. To its indignation it saw reflected on the surface the image of a ram equipped with a mighty pair of horns. Its reaction was immediate. Down went its head and at full speed it charged the supposed rival. The new window shattered into a thousand pieces and a very puzzled old tup stood marvelling at the enemy's sudden and total disappearance. At length it ambled away, doubtless to boast to the ewes of its pulverising power.

SQUIRRELS

View with Squirrels   by Donovan Clemson

From our British Columbian home we have an entrancing view of Shuswap Lake framed by two birch clumps 30 ft. apart. Their overhead limbs form a graceful arch of greenery in summer, a delicate tracery of fine twigs and catkins in winter. It would be impossible to place the two groups to better advantage; but for the numerous American red squirrels it is a different story. The general close growth of the trees assures a system of elevated trails over which they travel with ease, but the gap which provides our view introduces an uncertain element. Although the limbs of the two clumps approach each other to form an arch 25 ft. above the

161

ground, the slender outer twigs do not meet and are much too fine to support even a squirrel: the smallest leap is at least 6 ft. with a dubious landing opposite. Many times we have watched squirrels approach the gap and witnessed their agitation and, we believe, their cogitations. Some looked the situation over and descended to the ground, apparently preferring the possible indignity of being chased by our dogs to the risk involved in the jump. Others (or possibly the same ones, for we do not know them as individuals) have been more determined. Once a squirrel devoted a good five minutes to investigating the possibilities, creeping out on every likely limb until the twigs sagged, to make the gap even wider. After each inspection it returned to sit in a crotch, paws over palpitating heart, looking this way and that. It viewed the gap from the top of the tree, then descended almost to the ground, changed its mind and went back up again: to us it seemed to lack courage. Then it suddenly left its crotch, rushed up the trunk, tore along a projecting limb and hurled itself into the air. It crossed the gap, but the slender twigs offered no hold and its twisting body fell 20 ft. into a bushy young cedar. Before we had recovered from the shock, the victim had climbed the tree which was its objective and was continuing its tree-top route. On another occasion the problem was solved uniquely. The squirrel, after a routine of inspection and brief meditation, ascended the trunk to a chosen limb and nipped off all the foliage along it. As the leaves and twigs fluttered down, we realised that it was clearing an unobstructed run, to gain momentum for the big jump. The squirrel probably did not hear our applause as it took the approach at top speed. It made a splendid leap and landed in the opposite tree with ease.

Timely Insulation   **by Morven Waldron**

Once in early February my preparations for a bonfire were watched intently by the grey squirrels who live in our garden. A minute later I saw a sheet of 'The Daily Telegraph', with which I had planned to start the blaze, proceeding in a series of electric jumps up the trunk of our oak tree. At the top the squirrel dragged the paper into its drey, and a further six sheets were commandeered in this way. That night there was a heavy fall of snow.

Approaching a Double White Line by Dexter Watts

Approaching a double white line on a Cotswold road, I saw a grey squirrel appear and begin to undulate slowly across. I slowed to walking-pace, as did the driver of an oncoming lorry some fifty yards away. When the squirrel reached the white lines, it paused, jumped about eighteen inches up and over them and completed its leisurely crossing, completely ignoring both vehicles.

High-Rise Raider by Ruth E. S. Bell

For some weeks one winter dwellers in a large block of flats in Bournemouth had to keep their windows shut whatever the weather. It all started when a grey squirrel entered a sixteenth-floor window and found fruit and nuts on a table. It ate some of the fruit, but the nuts it deposited behind cushions or pushed down the sides of chairs, presumably to store them. Thus it set out on a house-breaking career, taking food and damaging soft and silky garments. It came from pine trees near by and ascended the huge building by going from balcony to balcony, reaching the first, about 10 ft. from the ground, by clinging to the roughcast wall. A friend of mine on the eleventh floor saw the squirrel running along the rail of her balcony, hastily shut all her windows and telephoned the people on the floor above to warn them that the creature was on the war-path. Another occupant was less fortunate; the thief entered, tore up a pair of nylon stockings, threw part of them out of the window and bundled out a pair of tights, which landed on the balcony beneath. One day my friend found her bedspread torn, mangled and twisted round the legs of a chair; the raider had apparently attempted to push it through the window. She tried to claim from her insurance company, but found that the policy did not cover depredations by squirrels. One day the window-cleaner gave the intruder a flick with his cloth to stop it entering by a window which was being cleaned from the inside. It tried to take a flying leap to the balcony above, missed and fell eleven floors into a puddle of water on concrete. The creature lay there, seemingly lifeless, for a quarter of an hour, then recovered, jumped up and ran away. One flat-dweller tried to make friends with it and was bitten for her pains. By mid January the flats were tyrannised no more: the squirrel had been shot by a gardener.

Swimming Squirrels   by M. G. Jolliffe

Half a dozen squirrels have been seen swimming a distance of at least 380 yards from Storholmen to Lidingö, one of the islands of the Stockholm archipelago. A similar incident was reported some twenty years ago when about fifty squirrels were observed to swim between the islands of one of the lakes of Central Sweden, probably to profit by the greater profusion of hazel bushes then on certain of the islands.

The Ways of Squirrels   by Eric Hardy

Having made a special study of red squirrels for many years – a colony lives not five minutes walk from my home – I was interested in the note on swimming squirrels at Stockholm in 'The Countryman'. How do squirrels hold their tails when they swim? I have seen near Liverpool squirrels swim and get their tails very wet, the result of the added water being that the squirrel promptly took to the nearest tree and sat on a bough shaking its tail until it dried. A swimming fox near Market Harborough got its tail wet in a similar manner: yet some nature books tell fanciful tales of how squirrel and fox hold their tails out of the water when they swim, to keep them dry. Has anyone else seen how a squirrel carries its tail in the water? Recently we saw an old doe squirrel take her young one by the scruff of the neck when a brown rat raided her nest, and carry it down the tree and along the ground to an old nest. I have seen red squirrels abroad an hour before daybreak on

Christmas morning when snow covered the ground and three degrees of frost was registered. A squirrel drinks every morning, lapping the water and hanging down the bank of the stream with the aid of its hind legs. In wet weather in winter squirrels often get their coats and tails very wet and cold and frequently sneeze and shiver; sometimes they cough, and when young, they are sometimes killed by the cold, wet weather, but never by cold alone. In summer I have found them abroad at 3 a.m. in the morning; never abroad after dusk. The courtship of squirrels often starts as early as January or February and young squirrels are sometimes born in April, though usually May, not coming out of the drey till June. There is much chasing and fighting in the court-ship, the buck and doe rolling over and over on the grass, squealing all the time, then chasing each other madly over the banks, round and round the boles. I once saw a squirrel bite another's ear off in courtship! A mated pair usually sticks together for life. I have known a wild red squirrel at least ten years.

A Grey Squirrel's Playthings   by Alan Duncan

Recently I saw an unusually large drey in the fork of a tree, and climbed up to examine it. I found that, although it must have been at least three years old, it had last been inhabited at some quite recent date. When I opened it a little I was surprised to find, in addition to the customary litter of a squirrel's nest, a small ball of coarse twine, an old and very tattered piece of cloth which appeared once to have been part of a shirt, a child's leather glove much marked by squirrels' teeth, several stones, part of a news-paper which the date proved to be eight months old, and two cigarettes. There were one or two other oddments, including the stub of a pencil and what appeared to be the ferrule of a walking-stick. But the prize of the whole collection was an ordinary bone cigarette-holder, much gnawed No attempt had been made to incorporate any of these things in the structure of the drey, except, oddly enough, the paper, which had been carelessly pushed into some crevices It appears, therefore, that the squirrel collected them only as playthings I have examined many other squirrels' nests and have never come across anything more uncommon than a scrap of paper or some stones.

Squirrel by Robert Gillmor

Bin for One   by Margaret Fisher-Rowe

Early one August morning I heard the familiar sound of the dust-bin lid being removed There was no wind and no-one from the house outside, so I looked out of the window A grey squirrel, the first I had seen since we came here some years ago, was standing against the bin and gently pushing up the lid with the top of its head. Then it moved the lid sideways until this was nicely balanced, whereupon it climbed up the bin and disappeared inside. A few minutes later it emerged to sit upright on top of the bin, where it began daintily to eat its booty, spitting out unwanted pieces all around. Then it slithered down and went through the gate on to the downs. It repeated this performance on several mornings at exactly the same time, until one day when I lifted the lid of the bin about noon to put in a can. There was the squirrel sitting at the bottom. I do not know which of us was the more surprised, but I have not seen it since, though a friend reports seeing one sitting outside our back door.

Joey   by Margaret Pickersgill

One autumn a grey squirrel took possession of our garden. We used to watch him nibbling acorns, and wondered where he came from. Then, one day at the end of November we saw him dart across the lawn, seize a white paper bag, bring it back along the fence and up the black poplar, and dive with it into the thick of the holly. Closer inspection showed a winter retreat of twigs and dry leaves, which Joey had built and was now upholstering. To what extent, we wondered, would he use the nest during the winter? Would he sleep for whole days, or even weeks? In November we had an early cold snap, with eleven degrees of frost, followed by a thick fog. We thought that Joey would surely sleep in on such a morning, but when we came downstairs we saw him in the oak. Again, in early January we had a thin covering of snow, but by breakfast time Joey's tracks were already everywhere. Throughout the winter he never missed a day.

We were interested, too, in the extent of Joey's territory. At first we thought that he did not wander beyond ours and the next-door garden, but later we found that he visited several gardens down the road and some nurseries still farther afield. When we plotted out his haunts they corresponded roughly to a square with sides a quarter of a mile long.

Visitors warned us that our garden would be ruined, but Joey left succulent daffodil shoots, budding crocuses and flowering aconites untouched. The children began to feed him by collecting a large basket of acorns; when these could no longer be found, they gave him an occasional chestnut. Then one day he arrived on the kitchen window-sill by way of the drain-pipe. We discovered that he enjoyed an occasional apple, but would not look at a tomato; toast was acceptable if he was hungry; but above all he loved cake.

When we put cake just inside the door, he comes in readily enough; and, as long as we do not attempt to approach within eighteen inches, he will sit on the kitchen mat eating while we have our meal. Perhaps the fact that he has only to ask and he is fed, either here or next door, has saved the gardens. I have seen him do damage only in moments of excitement; then sometimes he chews oak twigs, and only recently I watched him break off a branch of flowering currant by repeatedly leaping at it. He stores bread, cake and apples in a shallow hollow in the fork of the oak, or wedges them among a cluster of twigs or even in a crevice of a wall, and the birds know his tricks. As soon as he goes up the oak with a crust the sparrows gather just over his head. Before it has been in store for two minutes, starlings, sparrows and tits are helping to remove it.

At first all the cats in the neighbourhood were after Joey, and we were afraid that one of them would catch him unawares. But we didn't know Joey. He would come down the tree trunk towards the cat, which would creep nearer, then crouch with its tail moving slowly from side to side. Down he would come, farther and farther, until he was only four feet above the cat; then it would spring, but before it landed Joey was far out of reach on the nearest branch. Then he would run down the other side of the trunk, pick up an acorn and chew it nonchalantly on the ground beneath the cat, which eventually shuffled clumsily down. In the end he teased a cat one day, until it sprang; then he came quickly down the opposite side of the trunk until he was level with the cat, rushed round and repeatedly boxed its face very quickly with his fore-paws. The cat dropped five feet to the ground. Half an hour later the performance was repeated in the cherry tree. From that moment Joey began to get the upper hand. He would sit on the fence, while the cat tried to stalk him; all of a sudden he would leap like a little demon and the cat would fly in terror. Now the cats rarely come, though I twice saw one flee at full speed across the garden with Joey on its tail.

We laugh at many of his mannerisms. When alarmed he invari-

Engraving by William Wild

ably scratches himself with his hind leg; if in doubt whether to come on, he pauses a moment and fold his left fore-paw across his chest, for all the world like someone putting his hand to his heart. We laugh, too, when he goes wild playing tig with the trees,

169

rushing up the fence and down again, leaping among the low rhododendron branches, swaying on dead Michaelmas daisy stalks. All is done at lightning speed with twirling jumps that bring him facing down a tree when you think he is running up it. A hammock slung low between two fruit-trees provides the best game of all. He takes a running leap, swings for a moment, then lets go only to leap again; he does a hand-over-hand turn on it, runs all the way along it upside down, or right way up: he runs along, takes a leap straight up in the air, and comes down facing in the opposite direction. Delightful to watch, but impossible to describe! Now he has discovered that the children's climbing frame is ideal for a game. With perfect judgement he jumps clean through the space between the bars, runs round the bars, and up and down them, descends the rope of the swing and sits on the seat, and then climbs up into 'the tower' to survey the world before beginning all over again.

STOATS

Noises On and Off   compiled by B.C.

A neighbour was standing on the bridge which carries Akeman Street over the little river Glyme and looking towards a thick hedgerow along the slope. 'Seems like a ferret or maybe a white stoat', he said, and we could see something creamy-white undulating between the bushes. A stoat in ermine in Oxfordshire would indeed be an event, so my daughter and I entered the field to investigate. When I tried to approach the animal, which turned out to be a ferret on the loose, it disappeared down a rabbit-hole, popping up again almost immediately a few feet away. I made more overtures, torturing my lips to produce the sort of sucking noise with which I have sometimes stopped stoats and weasels in curiosity. But the ferret simply backed into the hole, uttering what I would describe as a quiet snarl.

This reminded me of something John Burton of the B.B.C.'s Natural History Unit saw on a sunny September day in Ashton

Park on the outskirts of Bristol. He had been demonstrating tape-recording techniques to Peter Corkhill, warden of the Skomer nature reserve, and his wife when they heard 'a loud bird-like squealing' coming from the vicinity of a fence. Under a gate two stoats were fighting furiously: 'they reared up on their hind legs and sparred with their forelegs, biting vigorously all the while'. After a minute or two they separated, but they had obviously been at it for several minutes before being spotted. Peter Corkhill switched on a tape-recorder, but the snatch of noise he picked up was spoilt, as is usual in Britain today, by the roar of cars on the road through the park. After breaking off the fight, one stoat chased the other up a narrow path alongside the fence, passing close to the observers before disappearing in woodland.

Two stoats fighting furiously by Robert Gillmor

171

According to the 'Handbook of British Mammals' stoats are usually silent; but when alarmed, both sexes give what is variously described as a 'bark' or a 'spitting rattle'. The only other stoat John Burton had heard to make a noise was one kept temporarily by Phil Drabble; he recorded it threatening a tame ferret. Its cry was a 'spitting snap', which may be much the same as the ferret's reaction. The handbook says of the ferret's nearest wild relative, the polecat, that it is 'normally silent but may utter series of short yelps and a variety of chattering and clucking noises'; and 'characteristic growling' has been noted during copulation. The weasel is credited with a varied voice, including a 'guttural hiss when alarmed' and a 'short screaming bark when provoked'.

It looks as though some clarification of the mustelid vocabularies is needed; and we now have a body organised to carry out special projects of this kind, the Wildlife Sound Recording Society. John Burton has been a moving spirit in it, and I have had the pleasure of speaking to its conference at the Woodchester Park field centre in the Cotswolds. Members are already studying the 'language' of foxes and badgers, and following up Terry Gompertz's classic analysis of the great tit's repertoire by recording some of its relatives, notably the puzzling willow tit and marsh tit.

A Head for Heights   by David Evans

We first saw the stoat crossing the lawn late one March evening. It was carrying by the nape of the neck a young rabbit which looked at least twice its own weight, back legs and bob-tail dragging the ground. Through the side of the bay window we watched the stoat ascend vertically the bare Virginia creeper on the front of the house, cross a ledge about 9 ft. up and continue nearly to the eaves, when suddenly the two bodies separated and plummeted to earth with audible thuds. Recovering quickly, the stoat picked up the rabbit again by the nape, walked back across the front of the house and round the side, and retraced its steps to the other side, apparently in search of an easier route Then it made a second assault on the creeper and rested with the rabbit on the ledge, before continuing its vertical path until it disappeared under the eaves and, we believe, into the attic. Our search revealed no nest, but there could easily be one somewhere in the 2-ft. Cotswold stone walls. We did not see the stoat again until early May when, in the gathering gloom of a thunderstorm, it followed the same path in front of the house, this time carrying a mouse up the creeper, over the ledge and into the eaves. It soon returned and, when we went into the garden, we discovered that it was coming from a small copse and crossing the road, the vegetable garden and the lawn, before attempting the climb, a total distance of about sixty yards. Seven times in twenty-five minutes we saw the stoat carry a mouse by this route, each time a little more hurried, probably because of the storm. The last two victims were larger than the rest and possibly the parents of the litter.

Rolling the Rabbit   by Christine A. C. Rae

Driving along a country road in Galloway, I saw a wriggling brown bundle appear from the grass verge. Stopping the car, I saw it was a stoat with an outsize rabbit, which it evidently wanted to take across the road. As the prey was too heavy to drag, the stoat stretched itself over the rabbit's body, took a firm grip with its teeth in the fur and skin and performed a forward roll, pulling the

rabbit with it. The stoat was now lying on its back underneath the carcase. Using its hind feet against the body to give leverage, it wriggled out, then repeated its actions. It continued this remarkable procedure until it reached the other side of the road with its prey and I lost sight of them in the long grass.

A Family of Stoats by R.H.C.

One July evening, as I was returning home by car, something started to cross the road about forty yards in front of me. It appeared to be a large brown snake, about four feet long and of exceptional thickness, moving towards the crown of the road in a series of twists and jerks. When, in a second or two, I reached the object, it divided in half, the front part continuing its journey across the road, and the rear portion doubling back on its tracks. Both halves disappeared into the grass verges and were lost to sight. Then I realised that I had seen a family of stoats, each holding on to the tail of the one in front.

Stoats' Family Dance by Dugald Macintyre

Watching from an ambush, I saw a family of twelve full-grown stoats follow their dam in Indian file down the ridge of an old turf dyke. Young stoats remain in the den where they were born until the males of the family are considerably larger than their mother. Then they are led out, and they quickly learn how to kill for themselves when the family scatters. Where the dyke ended, on a bare green patch, the stoats began to play and finally to dance. During the dance each member of the family was on its hind legs and had its mouth open, uttering those chuckling sounds which are also made by well-fed and contented families of ferrets. I was quite certain that this was merely dancing, and not at all designed to attract victims to their doom. Playful young ferrets which dance round their owners instead of setting to work are merely harmless nuisances until, the playful fit over, they close their mouths and get about their business.

174

page 175   *Short-tailed field vole*

page 176
(above) *A water vole photographed from a hide in Shropshire;*
(below) *fox*

TOADS

Enchanted Toad   by Kathleen M. Rowley

One dank autumn evening when we were living in a small cottage in the Forest of Dean, I opened the back door and saw a large dark toad squatting on the doorstep. It shuffled forward across a piece of fibre-mat, then over the matting of the kitchen floor to mount a shallow step into our sitting-room, when it crossed several yards of deep-pile carpet, coming to rest against the radio set. Our two sons, then aged twelve and seventeen, had the Light Programme switched on at all hours, so I cannot pretend that our toad had the cultured taste of the hare described in 'The Good Life', but it remained leaning against the set for a matter of hours. Before supper we decided to return it to the garden; but later, when I was about to lock up for the night, I again found a toad, apparently the same one, outside the back door. It embarked on the same journey over dry carpeted terrain to end up in its former position by the radio. We allowed it a further concert before returning it once more to the garden. Very late in the evening, to satisfy ourselves as to its intent, we opened the door again and in it came, to enjoy music till midnight. Finally we carried it carefully more than 60 yds. up the garden, where it made a permanent home for the next three years.

WATER VOLES

Why so Black?   compiled by B.C.

Beatrix Potter did not immortalise the water vole, nor has it attracted adverse attention from pest-control scientists in Britain, where it does little damage to crops or river banks; on the Continent it is much more of a nuisance. Here it remains a relatively unknown, though often abundant, member of our fauna. It poses two problems of interest to D. M. Stoddart, who has made the water vole his special study. One concerns coat colour which is predominantly black in Scotland north of the Trossachs-Tay line

(97 per cent against 3 per cent brown). In the south, on the other hand, water voles are normally brown, although there are black populations in the Cambridgeshire Fens and in Norfolk. Since they are diurnal and known to be preyed on by several mammals, birds and fish, one would expect black to be a dangerous colour for the voles. Dr Stoddart wondered whether it was of advantage in cold climates, but examination of pelts right across Europe to Lake Baikal gave no support to this idea. Perhaps black is linked genetically to another characteristic of sufficient survival value to outweigh the disadvantage.

The second problem concerns scenting, by which water voles mark the boundaries of their ranges. On each flank just in front of the hind leg, they have a gland which produces a sweet musk. Dr Stoddart hopes to elucidate what happens when one vole finds another's scent mark. This must often occur, as the ranges of four out of five males overlap. Does the second run away or lay its own scent on top? By laying artificial odours it may be possible to upset the territorial organisation and confuse the voles, so that their reactions can be studied. This research may produce ideas for the control of rats and mice, which have more diffuse scent glands.

WEASELS

A Varied Diet   by Ann Campbell

Seeing the bird-table deserted and the tall macrocarpa hedge alive with apprehensive birds, I looked from the window to the far end of the garden and saw a weasel snaking its way towards the house. Its progress through the drift of oak leaves against the hedge showed only as a rippling wave and occasional flash of white underparts. A few yards from the house it peered from the leaves before dashing out to reconnoitre. Round and round the bird-table it raced in ever-widening circles, avoiding clumps of grass and fruit bushes with athletic skips and twists of its supple body. Now and again it stopped to sit up on hind legs, darting quick

178

glances all round. Suddenly it ran up the 4-ft. pole of the table and negotiated the overhang by letting go with its front paws, leaning back momentarily, then grasping the edge and hoisting itself up and over in the manner of a looper caterpillar. Once on the table it grabbed a piece of boiled potato in its mouth and was back on the ground in no time, running down the pole head first. The weasel concealed itself behind a tussock of dry grass, but I could look down and watch it eating. Several blackbirds had become so curious that they descended to lower branches; but their neurotic clamour was ignored by the animal, which was soon on the table again, this time to eat rolled oats. It sat there, 6 ft. from the window, its short tail hanging over the edge. Two house sparrows, bolder than the rest, fluttered over the uninvited guest. This all happened at midday one January 11th, but the weasel had been visiting the vicinity of my bird-table for more than five months. Sometimes it had come once or even twice a day; then it was not seen for several weeks. At first it had been content to eat fallen food, but one day it had climbed a black-currant bush near by and, swaying on the whippy branches, stretched upwards to see what was on the table. Realising that better pickings were to be had, it had begun its efforts to climb the pole and had at first been frustrated by the overhang of the tray. But persistence, second nature to weasels, had eventually been rewarded, and it was seen to eat bread, toast, rolled oats, boiled potato, hard-boiled egg, fried fish, fat, liver and odds and ends of raw and cooked meats. Its immaculate condition, alertness, mobility and strength seemed to discount the possibility that it had adopted this diet because of damaged teeth or old age. Nor is there any lack of natural prey in this area of Thetford Chase. Was it simply an individualist, or is the weasel's diet more varied than 'The Handbook of British Mammals' suggests?

[Perhaps a bit of both; in Spring 1963 S. R. Davidson recorded a stoat taking suet from a Perthshire bird-table. *B.C.*]

To and Fro   **by Douglas Carr**

We were sitting in the car outside Swyncombe Church, near Ewelme in Oxfordshire, at 12.30 one August day when a weasel ran out of the churchyard and across the road, carrying what appeared to be a full-grown long-tailed field mouse. It returned at 12.35 without the mouse, and at 12.45 dashed over with a second. During the next 56 minutes it brought out five more mice and what looked like a young rat about 4 in. long excluding the tail. Some-times it took only three minutes to make a capture, but its final visit to the churchyard occupied nearly 18 minutes and it emerged at 1.41 without prey. We waited another 50 minutes, but did not see the weasel again.

Death on the Ice   **by William A. Woodrow**

Three days and nights of frost had sealed the drains and flashes of the Norfolk marsh. The tidal river had coated fringes and fronds of vegetation, looking like crystallised angelica. The ice was thickest in the cutting up to the boat-house, where I broke it twice a day and scattered corn so that the waterfowl might come to feed in relative safety. The boat-house itself provided an excellent hide. It was a regular feature of the landscape and therefore inconspicuous; it offered protection from the bone-splitting east wind and gave me a good view of the birds which flocked to the spot. These were mainly moorhens, mallard and teal with an occasional coot and once a great crested grebe. But I was too visible; in spite of their hunger the birds were wary, and any sound, amplified in that still frosty air, sent them off at once. Unlike wild geese, they did not keep a watchman. All seemed to feed avidly, yet at a signal unnoticed by me they would disperse on the instant, the duck flying off, the coots and moorhens waddling away to the river's open water.

A slight chill kept me indoors for a night and a day while it continued to freeze. After tea I wrapped up and went out again with a crowbar; as I expected, the cutting was frozen over. What I did not expect, though I had heard of its happening, was to see a bird captured by the ice. It was a teal, held by legs and tail feathers, and it seemed to be dead. In the shadow of the boat-house I wondered what to do; the ice was too thin to bear me. Then I heard a high-pitched squeaking from the reeds, like an unoiled brake or mice in the walls of an old cottage. It went on and on until the withered stems parted and a weasel writhed out into the open. It stepped daintily, sniffed the air, paused, looked behind for an instant, then lunged its head and neck forward towards the captive teal. Two others followed.

Warily the three tiny creatures came to the cutting's edge. The leader touched the ice with a tentative paw and drew back. It moved forward again cautiously on to the surface, followed by the other two. They had obviously scented the teal and hunger drew them on. As, with a curious weaving side-stepping gait, they came nearer, the teal moved. Fear had conquered exhaustion, and it made frantic efforts to pull free.

Not more than two feet from the bird the first weasel suddenly reared up, quite vertical, sitting on its tail like an otter. Once more came the quiet squeaking as it began to weave about, with head, shoulders and fore-paws all moving. The others, about two feet behind, began to mimic this but neither was able to stay erect with the same freedom and grace. On all fours again, the weasels began to circle clockwise round the teal, then stopped. More weaving before they reversed and ran counter-clockwise. They stopped, weaved and reversed again and again until a definite rhythm was built up. This seemed to hypnotise the teal; it gave up tugging at the ice and sat, beak agape, rotating its head as the weasels ran around and about it.

Suddenly they all halted, as if some silent signal had passed, and retreated almost to the edge of the cutting where they lay flat, their russet coats contrasting with the leaden colour of the ice. The leader began to work forwards again, while the other two lay watching. The teal watched too, but exhaustion overcame it once more and it gradually sank on to the ice. Nearer came the weasel until almost within touch. Then it reared up on its tail, slowly this

181

time, and the teal rose with it, until the two creatures, the tiny predator and the much larger bird, were both at full stretch and facing each other. The weasel darted, caught the teal by the throat and the two collapsed together. Again the impression of a silent signal and the other weasels pounced. Between them they tore the teal from the ice. The leader gripped it and with a curious shake, like a dog with a rabbit or an old glove, dragged the prey off into the reeds, followed by the others.

Jim Vincent, formerly gamekeeper on the Horsey estate, a few miles to the north, told me that he had once seen weasels take a teal in a hard winter before the war. But the interest lies not so much in the unusual prey as in the reason for their behaviour in the preliminary stages. They may have been carrying out a sequence that is part of the ritual of the kill. Once started, they were virtually unable to change it, because it is a genetically determined pattern for weasels on the hunt. There are other interpretations. The most likely is that the weasels, facing a situation outside their normal experience, had to improvise a plan of campaign and were working themselves up to a pitch at which they could attack their large prey with impunity.

Deceit or Disease?   compiled by B.C.

Timothy is a cat living at Broughton in Peeblesshire. One summer's day he carried a weasel into the kitchen and laid it at his mistress's feet. She asked her husband what she should do with it. ' "Put it in the burn," was the terse reply', as reported to me by Eleanor Quin of Edinburgh, who continued: 'She accordingly scooped up the corpse on a shovel . . . and tipped it into the burn that flows past her fence. No sooner had the weasel tumbled into the water than it sprang to life, dashed to the opposite bank and streaked away across the field. Was it acting dead, or truly hurt and revived by immersion?'

I could find nothing relevant in the standard works on British mammals, but struck oil when I asked Michael Stoddart of the

Animal Ecology Research Group at the Department of Zoology at Oxford. His colleague Carolyn King has been collecting accounts of unusual behaviour by stoats, weasels and their relatives, and has six records of 'shamming dead' by weasels, three published and three sent to her personally. They have one point in common : the animals passed out after a period of high excitement or shock, and in three cases cats were involved. One of them (also called Tim) brought in a weasel on three separate occasions. Another intervened in a running fight between two weasels; the pursuer ran for a hedge, and the pursued into the jaws of the cat, who must have dropped it on the approach of the observer. The third cat, like Timothy of Broughton, offered its prey to Mrs M. Thomson, and the 'supposedly dead sprang to life' as she was examining it.

The three other observations are quite dissimilar. In his book 'A Weasel in My Meatsafe' (Collins 1957) Phil Drabble described the temporary black-outs of his tame Teasy, who had the run of the living-room; they were apparently brought on by violent exertion, and eventually the animal died. J. D. Powne of Dorset intervened in a fight between a stoat and a weasel, which seemed to be unconscious. He put it in a sack and took it home, where it eventually revived quite quickly and made off. Finally comes a remarkable incident seen by K. Spink in Derbyshire in May 1955: 'Three sparrows were tormenting a young weasel, taking it in turns to pretend to be injured, trailing their wings in front of it and then jumping out of reach. The weasel made fitful short rushes at the birds; but after about fifteen minutes it seemed incapable of further movement and lay motionless in the road.' When examined, 'it was apparently in good condition, mouth wide open and breathing deeply', but the muscles seemed to be tensed. When Mr Spink retired some distance, 'the sparrows resumed their dangerous game'.

Carolyn King takes the view, which I strongly support, that 'if an incident is described sufficiently often by independent observers, there is a fair chance that it qualifies as a pattern of behaviour occasionally shown by the species'; but its meaning remains to be interpreted. My first thought on reading Eleanor Quin's letter was to relate her weasel's behaviour to shamming dead by young birds of prey and the adult injury-feigning and distraction displays which have survival value in deceiving a predator. Carolyn King points out that cats maul and eat dead prey, and there is no apparent reason why they should treat a lifeless weasel differently; so it would be risky to counterfeit death. But I am not entirely convinced that a shamming animal might not get a chance to bolt when dropped by a cat; Mrs Thomson's account certainly suggests the possibility. On the other hand stoats, weasels and other mustelids suffer from a parasitic worm *Skjrabingylus*, which lodges in the skull between and behind the eyes. It does considerable damage, producing deformations which must exert great pressure on the brain. Carolyn King suggests that this may be 'the direct cause of the temporary blackout in moments of stress.' Little is known of the life history of the parasite, which she and others are now studying. 'If it can be shown,' she continues, 'that the area where pressure is greatest is that part of the brain wholly or partly concerned with consciousness, there may be some support for the hypothetical correlation'.

She very fairly admits that the reported incidents vary in detail. The body may be rigid or limp, very still or twitching; and the observers may have been describing different phenomena. Nevertheless she feels that, 'on the balance of available evidence, it seems reasonable to conclude that weasels do not "sham dead" in the sense of staging a deliberate deception, but that they are susceptible to sudden attacks of genuine unconsciousness', possibly due to infection by a destructive cranial parasite. But supposing the unconsciousness does confer an advantage in deceiving enemies, may this be why *Skjrabingylus* persists? Symbiosis between host and parasite is a feature of nature; so is a balance of advantage. The conspicuous plumage of many male birds may be fatal to them, but is sufficiently advantageous when securing a mate to persist in all its dangerous glory.

Witherets **by Jane King, Elinor Handford and E. V. Malone**

We were looking for standing stones on the slopes of Slieve Snaght in Donegal. The farmer, a man of about forty, was welcoming and helpful. No, he had not heard of standing stones thereabouts, but in one of the fields there was a stone that had caught the ploughshare so often that his father had taken it up. They had found an underground tunnel, and his uncle had gone down with a torch.

'I'd be feart to go down there meself,' he admitted. 'I'd be feart o' them witherets. That's a class o' wee animal like a rat, an' that's not got a bone till its body. Ye meet one o' them witherets an' that'll put its tail between its teeth an' whizzle at ye. An' if ye go to heave a stone at a witheret that'll never leave ye. I'm tellin' no lie. That'll stay with ye for the rest of your days. Ay, that's a wee kind o' beast like a stoat, ye know, an' there's never a bone till its body. I'd be feart to meet them witherets.'

We came back to investigate, and found a tunnel 58 ft. long that might be 3000 years old; but we met no witheret. *Jane King*

[Dr Katharine Briggs comments: 'There is a widely recorded dialect word, "wittret", "whitrack", etc., meaning weasel or stoat. Though there are no weasels in Ireland, the word is used there for the stoat, and in Lady Wilde's "Ancient Legends of Ireland" it is an uncanny creature which it is bad luck to try to kill. Both animals "whistle", and their supple movements could suggest bonelessness.']

One summer an old County Antrim pensioner warned me never to interfere with a 'witheret', as they were most dangerous and never forgot. He told me of a man who killed one which ran across his path and, some time later on the same path, was attacked by several so fiercely that he had to run for it. *Elinor Handford*

A County Down farm worker claims to have been chased by a pack of 'weasels' one May just outside Castlewellan Forest Park; he estimated their number as about 20 and says that they chased him for fully 60 yards. *E. V. Malone*

Taming a Weasel   by J. C. Bristow-Noble

One morning a cat brought an old male weasel into the house and laid him on the floor. He appeared quite lifeless, but when the cat gave him a poke with a paw, he sprang up like a flash and seized her by the nose, bull-dog fashion. Amazed and terrified by the suddenness of it all, she shook him off and fled.

I had never handled a live weasel before, and hastily put on a pair of kid gloves. The little animal faced me, standing on his hind legs, his mouth open and coat bristling, hissing and spitting like an angry kitten. When I stooped to pick him up, he sprang on to my leg and began to bite my trousers. Although I took firm hold of him round the neck, close up to the head, he had no difficulty in biting my fingers, but I could only just feel his small teeth through the gloves.

I put him into a canary breeding-cage and gave him a little bread and milk in a saucer. He made a good meal, eating slowly and daintily. Then I placed the cage in the sun, and he lay at full length and slept long and soundly. When he awoke I gave him a nest of dead grass and small feathers. This he arranged to his liking, making it rounder and more compact, before curling up in it.

Meanwhile I had been able to get a freshly killed mouse and two sparrow's eggs. As soon as I held the mouse inside the cage, he came forward cautiously, grabbed the food and backed into the nest. In a few moments he came out again to the eggs, which I had broken into a saucer, and lapped up the two small yolks. He then spent some minutes grooming himself, and returned to the nest. For a long time I could hear him crunching up the mouse. The following morning all that remained of it were the feet and tail. The hair, I noticed, he had scratched off the skin and added to the lining of his nest. I offered him more bread and milk, but he drank only a little of the milk and ignored the bread. He groomed his chestnut coat methodically with his small pink tongue, and then romped about the cage, jumping and rolling, before having another long sleep in the sun.

In a week's time he was tame. He would come fearlessly to the door of the cage for his food and take it gently out of my hand. A mouse or sparrow in the evenings, and a little bread and milk or water in the morning, with an occasional titbit – a small piece of chicken liver or a little raw egg – during the day, was food enough for twenty-four hours.

Presently I let him out of the cage in my study. I closed the door and windows, placed the cage on the floor, opened its door, called and waited. He was soon at the door, but minutes passed before he ventured further. At last he stepped sedately out and sat grooming his coat. Gradually he made a timid exploration of the room, broken now and again by a lighning sprint back to his nest. When he had looked into every corner, he began to play and stalk flies. He rushed here and there, hopping and jumping, his stumpy tail in the air, rolling and tossing himself about like an acrobat in the circus ring, until he was tired and out of breath. Then he stretched himself on his back in the sun. After about an hour I got up rather noisily from my chair and, instantly, with a squeal and hiss, he rushed back to his cage.

I continued to let him out every day for a romp, as he became tamer and more trusting. When I called him he would come to me and allow me to stroke his head and pick him up; if he was tired, he would fall asleep on my lap. At this stage of his domestication, he became inquisitive. He would climb up on my lap uninvited, pop in and out of my jacket pockets, crawl up the sleeves and come out at my neck, and then go back to the floor, only to return and go over the same ground again. He was very puzzled on one occasion when I lay back in the chair and closed my eyes. He jumped lightly on my face and tried first to lick the eyelids open and then to open them with his feet.

When I had had him for two months, I had to leave the country for London, so I put the cage in some shrubs in the garden, opened the door and left him. At the time he was asleep in the nest. It was

187

Weasel by Kenneth Underwood

a good hour before he came out and, when he did so, he came at once into the house, climbed up me and curled himself in one of my jacket pockets. In the evening I took him back to the cage with a freshly killed three-weeks-old rabbit and some water.

On the following morning I found him still asleep in the nest, and more than half of the rabbit was still uneaten. He did not awake till late afternoon. After coming into the house and remaining with me an hour or so, he went back to finish the rabbit, which was nearly all gone the next morning; he was then fast asleep again. That evening he came into the house, chiefly, I think, to see what I had for his supper. I gave him some milk, and nothing more. I could see that he was hungry but he knew that there were shrews and mice in the shrubs near the cage. He left me and began to hunt. A little later he was in the cage eating a mouse.

From now on I gave him only water. Two days before I left, I took the cage away and put him into a rat-hole beneath a corn rick about a hundred yards from the shrubbery. He popped quickly down the hole, and in a few moments I heard a rat or rats scrambling up into the rick. He soon caught a mouse and brought it to the shrubs but, finding that the cage was gone, took it back to the rick.

That was the last I saw of him, as I left the following day. I was told he came to the house a few times but, not finding me there, hustled back at once to the rick. When this was threshed some two months later a weasel, presumably my friend, bolted from it into a rat-hole in the bank.

WILD CATS

Once seen . . .   **by Kathleen Pateman**

After sitting all morning at our favourite bay, two miles beyond Durness in Sutherland, at about half-past one we decided to go back to the village. As we were driving along I saw a buzzard, which dropped quickly to the rocks at the foot of the mountain on our left. We stopped and I searched with the glasses, until I found something which seemed to be huddled motionless against a grey rock. I was wondering whether it was all right, when suddenly it turned its head and revealed itself as a huge cat. It was looking straight at our car from about 300 yds. away. We sat for more than half an hour, waiting for it to move; but it just lay there watching us, paws tucked in and only its eyes blinking. My husband decided to walk along a loose rock wall towards it, and from his first step the cat watched him, turning its head a little sideways. Finally, as he was getting fairly near, it jumped over the boulder with a tremendous spring and streaked up the mountainside. I saw the huge body, the flat ears and the ringed tail perfectly; and, as if to give me good measure, the wild cat stopped again, looked round, then bolted off, up and up, round a shoulder of the mountain and out of sight.

WILD LIFE

Gorongosa   by Charlotte Truepeney

Our African courier-driver is earnest about an early start. He appears at first light, imploring us not to linger over breakfast under the trees. He is not satisfied until his bus load is checked out of the wire-enclosed camp and he has begun his day-long effort to please. Every passenger is taut with expectation, nose to window. We are inside a hundred square miles of wild-animal territory – inside Gorongosa, the National Park of Mozambique. It shows us nothing but its rags, the tatty end of winter – the season without rain: grass turned to straw, despairing saplings, palms rising a hundred feet in dilapidation. As we penetrate deeper and deeper into the African bush, it reveals nothing.

Would-be wild-life viewers burst out, 'Where are the buck?' 'What about zebra?' 'We must have lions.' My own wish is to see, in addition to every possible animal, the fabulous sausage tree. Gradually the bush is succeeded by open plain; then it happens.

Excitement explodes as the courier triumphantly cries, 'We see waterbucks now, all bucks, impala.'

'Where? Where? Oh, look!' Only after searching wildly, the untrained eye beholds the herds blending distinctly into the plain – to us an immense number of horned, almost magical creatures.

'Few only,' says the courier and stops the bus. 'Fire has eaten grass.' Great herds can be seen covering the plain in April after the rains. 'We see now wildebeeste.'

Amazed, speechless, we stare. So strange a beast can only have come out of Africa, a queer heraldic shape with a touch of unicorn. He belongs truly to Gorongosa, contributing his part to her embracing atmosphere of primeval mystery. Breaking into a canter, in threes and fours, they make speed, heads low, heavy shoulders thrusting, the long manes floating – dull-coloured creatures, like the shadows which soon consume them. How close they came!

The wildebeeste jubilation has scarcely died down when the courier says, 'We see now warthog.' Trotting prettily like miniature horses, a couple come out of a spur of bush. Suddenly they turn monstrous snouts towards us, ugly as sin, then dash on, tails vertical – flags of defiance.

Rivulets, low in water, begin to appear. A sharp-eyed viewer sees a fish eagle in white feather surplice; someone else the marabou stork. Pelicans lift gross beaks to each other. The lady who longs for lions is downcast: 'Half the morning gone.' Nor is my sausage tree anywhere to be seen. The plain becomes dried out marshes, open and endless under the African sky, always more vast and vital than any other sky. So down to the river itself, as great as a sea, where the wind blows hard and fifty dark islands with pink streaks submerge and rise up – as hippopotami.

Everyone spills out of the bus, but the courier forbids standing at the water's edge. A hippo weighing a ton can dash to attack the unarmed viewer, as it will dash from the river to stamp out a fire. Rising imperceptibly from the water, one island becomes a large hippo moving with awesome sloth towards the herd; his head seems to split in two as his jaws part and he speaks: hardly a roar,

'Heavy shoulders thrusting, the long manes floating'

yet more than a grunt. Noses like pink port-holes bunching in friendly converse quiver apart; the river ripples as the master approaches.

The longing for lions has now infected the whole party. We look for them in vain; and we look for the sausage tree till we are sure it was invented by Lear. Flat and blank, the plain takes us back to the bush; the morning is over, all hope of lions lost. Suddenly the courier leaves the track, and the bus stops in the grass.

A lioness has spread herself in the shade, one paw flung out across a smooth brown stone. She is painted into her background; the brown, the yellow and darkness of the winter veld reflected in the coat. Small pieces of raw meat strewn gruesomely around give a reminder of her tastes. She turns to blink mildly at the bus, completely indifferent to our presence; she has smelt only petrol and this does not disturb her. Carefully the courier brings the bus closer. The raw meat turns into crimson flowers, and the brown stone into a vast Vienna sausage – the fallen pod of Lear's own tree.

Embarrassment of riches! There, at a few yards, lies the queen of beasts, and above her the sausage tree itself showering blossoms on her: a well-shaped smallish tree, the lower branches scarcely

192

'Trotting prettily'

able to carry the occasional mature pod. More than two feet long and many inches thick, some of these gross appendages have dropped to lie about like sleeping animals.

No-one is allowed to alight. The flowers of the sausage tree remain ungathered, a carpet for a lioness. Later, and not in the presence of lions, I pick one up. A large peculiar cup, blood red, with scalloped lips turned back, dark stripes within pointing the way no doubt to a reservoir of sweetness – a butt of Malmsey for a bee.

One lion is not enough. We beg the courier for more. Obediently seeking, he noses the bus along the track close to ant-hills crowned by trees – often a lion look-out – and thickets heavy with creepers; we peer into the black midday shadows from which only a car full of elated viewers emerges, in reverse. Our lion-minded group is poised for a pride or even a kill. Tension rises, and continues to rise as the bus proceeds still more softly until, caught in the hot silence, it comes to a halt; an elephant engaged in picking fruit straddles the road. Smaller grey backs stand under the branches while he rocks the tree lightly with his trunk, and fruit rains down on the family. Little trunks feel in the grass for it and pop it into wide red mouths. Then father lifts his tattered ears like large banana leaves; he is no longer indifferent to us. We watch him, wrapped in the study. Ponderous movements in the stillness, the snap of a twig, a bird singing, hard sunlight, deep shade, the flash of dropping fruit. Happily absorbed, a teenage elephant and two babies go on gathering the 'sweeties' shaken down for them. The banana-leaf ears flap meaningly. Did a quiver run through the loose and wrinkled skin of the adult male? Gear in reverse, foot on clutch, the courier has kept the engine running. Now we begin to slide gently backwards, leaving the elephant family to continue their repast.

An afternoon without lions has its compensations: baboons dropping like airborne troops, not from the sky but from the branches, their close clever eyes observing us; jostled trees marking the progress of a string of elephant, glimpsed forms moving in dark immensity, single file, all sizes, through the forest; the sabi star or impala lily, a solitary gem in the veld, like a small baobab, lifting smooth leafless arms bearing the starlike flowers edged with red; the hasty return of enthusiastic photographers as the courier hustles them into the bus at the sight of approaching buffalo; the mass of dark bodies, the light-catching horns and the heavily armoured foreheads; a single waterbuck grazing close enough for us to see the curious patches of brilliant colour about his head; lastly, in the heart of Gorongosa, a forest of spells and dreams.

The track enters the precincts of a ghostly host robed in yellow. We mingle with these beings, beautiful and repellent in pale chrome, trunk and branch, one unvarying colour, a sameness rare in nature.

'Their close clever eyes observing us'

'Dis is fever tree,' says the courier. 'I tell you mosquito is giving me fever, not tree. Dat is so.'

Another and another high, yellow-boned tree, fanning graciously at the head with twigs like jaundiced fingers ringed with flowers. Trees of witchcraft, to the early settlers trees of ague, graceful purveyors of disease and death – nightmare trees. Lit now by sunlight, golden angel trees, forming Gothic shapes with the upward thrust of boughs eager for heaven. Atmosphere lies heavy over all Gorongosa; in the yellow forest it becomes a presence.

195

'The queen of beasts, and above her the sausage tree'

The silence is carefully preserved. People who wish for loud music and late nights, with a few wild animals thrown in, do not come to Gorongosa. The curfew is strict; at 10 p.m., when the camp's generator cuts out, darkness descends; candles are provided but visitors who breakfast at dawn are already asleep. The speed limit of 18 m.p.h. must be observed; anyone who runs down an animal is bitingly reprimanded, fined and expelled from the camp. To disturb the animals is sacrilege; the rule of regard for them is enforced. They respond by coming forth fearlessly. Some wild-life reserves in southern Africa have suffered through the behaviour of visitors; the animals tend to remain in hiding. Observers have reported simple facts: that lions resent having oranges thrown at them; that giraffes are terrified by shrill laughter, loud voices and so on.

Gorongosa is the creation of a young man who guards his kingdom of nature passionately. Alfredo Rodrigues, a wiry bearded Portugese with quiet charm and an unobtrusive manner, is unmarried, devoting his life to the Park.

'You like the Park?' His face brightens with a pleasure which he must have had so many times but of which he never wearies – praise of the park. Someone inquires about poaching.

'The poaching is very much; we must guard all the time. Both black and white men are coming to kill elephant for the meat. But now it is less because the government punishes the poachers. The punishment is terrible, but so is the poaching. It is terrible.'

All the creatures we have seen are protected day and night by the master and his rangers. They also guard the grass, the fever trees, the sausage tree, the sabi star, the reptiles, the insects, the birds and the very mystery of Gorongosa.

On our second and last morning the cry for lions is frantic; we have seen only one. The courier drives us to the old rest camp, now taken over by lions, he says – and to disappointment. There is no impressive form sleeping like a dog on the doorstep; no leonine face at a window; only swallows sweep screaming through the doorless huts. Wherever one looks today the animals' kingdom is blank and secret. It has turned hot as, at funereal pace, burying our last hope of lions, we take the road for the exit. Even at the 18 m.p.h. speed limit we shall soon reach the main gates, and the white pole will lift for our return to the world of men. Unpredictable Gorongosa! At this farewell moment she throws us her plum.

Of course, no-one sees them at first, for they belong to the shadows which shelter their retirement under the trees. The stately manner abandoned, a dozen have relaxed. Just zoo animals? Described by early travellers, seen in medieval drawings, endlessly photographed today, the greatest personality among wild creatures, master of them all, this beast has always excited human admiration. Scorning to kill for pleasure, he kills inexorably for food. The female, with deadly cunning, drives the prey towards her mate for his lethal spring; there is no escape. Only man may hunt this hunter.

Farther north luxuriant black manes are worn, but here the

'No longer regal but merely overcome with heat'

shorter gingery mane suffices; even so the males lie panting. No longer regal but merely overcome with heat, nearly all lie on their backs, paws in air, mouths open, uninhibited and snoring grandly. We have caught the royal creatures *en pantoufle*.

A small buck grazes twenty yards away, unafraid of resting kings sated with food. Two wakeful cubs begin to stalk it; the mother stirs and by a soundless command sends them to cover in the bushes. She falls asleep again. An old hunter with scars on his head and a weeping eye rouses to look with equal boredom at the bus and the near-by buck. He blinks, his head droops and, like the rest, the veteran slumps into sleep. For them the sleep of the fearless; for us a grand finale of lions.

Drawings by Charlotte Truepeney

Africa for Everyman   by Bruce Campbell

Take one stately home, complete with assorted mature trees, a couple hundred acres of grassland, and one or more ornamental lakes. Separate the grassland into irregular areas bounded by high fences, encircling the whole with a barbed wire zareba; lay down circuitous metalled roadways to taste, add a mixture of cafés, lavatories, zoovenir shops and ice-cream kiosks. Fill each compound carefully with exotic fauna, garnish with attractive flowerbeds, sprinkle with bush-hatted keepers and warning notices, invite the Press to a preliminary tasting, and your safari park or wild-life park is ready for public consumption.

This recipe had already been concocted successfully when I wrote about the zoo explosion two and a half years ago and in spite of rising prices for everything – a giraffe may set you back £1500 before it can be added to the attractions – the demand shows no signs of slackening; indeed, with the big circus firms behind them, new variations of the dish are constantly emerging.

The Federation of Zoological Gardens of Great Britain and Ireland makes no distinction between a zoo and a wild-life park: one shades into the other. But such consumer research as I have been able to do suggests that to the public they embody different concepts. A zoo has cages and you walk round them looking at the animals; in a wild-life park the animals are much freer and may even walk or fly round you. The profession, if that is what it now is, seems to be making a further sub-division, reserving the term 'safari park' for a lay-out which includes a 'jungle drive' in a closed car past some of the reputedly fiercer or more mischievous African fauna, with zebra-striped landrovers strategically placed to come to the rescue if needed. The anticlimax is provided by the stars themselves: after a recent visit to one of the largest of these establishments in the country I cannot recall seeing a single lion or

cheetah with its eyes open as I churned decorously along in bottom gear.

Actually, this was very much as I saw their wild relatives behave in the reserves of East Africa, and at British safari parks there is not a surge of minibuses to watch a pride of lions enjoying their latest kill. In Nairobi's National Park an utterly indifferent lion and lioness chewed a wildebeeste surrounded by sixteen vehicles, whose occupants were completely frustrated in their efforts to secure 'natural' photographs of the royal pair. But in other respects there is a close resemblance between the Nairobi park and its British copies; baboons leave their finger-prints on your car as they explore in the faint hope that you will disregard the rule against feeding them. Hunched marabou storks and vultures do not reveal their pinioned state, and our own house sparrows are not so different from the grey-headed sparrows of Kenya. This, I suppose, is why our safari parks continue to attract their tens of thousands, since they no longer have the novelty that attended the opening of Longleat in 1966, when the Marquess of Bath and Jimmy Chipperfield 'established the first reserve for lions in the western world', as Geoffrey Schomberg puts it in his invaluable Penguin 'Guide to British Zoos'.

So far the lions have done little to arouse pleasurable frissons of anticipation among the occupants of the crawling motorcades. It is ironic that the ox-like eland should have been responsible for the recent fatal accident at Woburn and a giraffe for an incident at newly-opened Knowsley Park. The giraffes at Blair Drummond, at present Scotland's only safari park, range freely among the visitors, ogling them with those preposterous eyelashes; it is this freedom, as well as the association with wildest Africa, that attracts the public.

On the other hand, when writing recently about Glasgow's Linn Park, I mentioned that a small collection of caged birds provided a valuable focus of interest for both children and adults, and at all the parks I have visited there are aviaries, vivaria for reptiles, and usually some mammals in cages. Often these exhibits are not properly labelled, which exasperates me but does not worry most visitors. 'What are those dark things down there?' asked a lady at St. Leonard's Park near Windsor, pointing to what I took to be California quails. But she did not seem to expect an answer to her question.

Snakes, it seems, fascinate even when comatose. 'Old John used to come to school with one inside his shirt', a young man told his girl companion with vicarious pride in the darkness of a small reptile house. Many curators, like Brian Sinfield of the Cotswold Wild-life Park at Bradwell near Burford, believe that a variety of easily-seen animals is essential to build up an initial interest, and that specialisation should follow when the park has become an established attraction with a regular clientele. This will help con-servation, both by building up stocks for release in the original habitat and for exchange with other institutions.

A feature of the Cotswold park brochure is the list of wild birds and mammals that have been observed there recently, and I believe that this aspect could be greatly developed, though not every park can expect to emulate the Wildfowl Trust at Slimbridge and have several hundred Bewick's swans turn up faithfully each winter outside the Honorary Director's studio. The remark-able oscillations that many birds show between tameness and wildness pose a problem animal behaviour students have still to crack, and wild-life parks may well have their contribution to make. At Bradwell there is a gannet which was picked up in the neighbourhood over a year ago, evidently storm-driven. It was put with the penguins and appears to have identified itself with them, for it makes no attempt to fly away and takes no more notice of the visitors than they do.

Although we have a very high proportion of commercially-run zoos and wild-life parks, many of them take their educational res-ponsibilities as seriously as those owned by scientific societies. At Bradwell there are now residential courses of a week for children between 8 and 13, run by Michael Molesworth, who makes full use of the surroundings in which the animals live. One project, for example, involves the study of a deciduous tree and asks thirty-five questions to which the child has to find answers during the year. The bird project asks eighty-five questions and answers involve tape-recording songs and calls, while the camera is used to make a photographic record of behaviour. Other subjects can be linked to botany and zoology: the volume of an ancient oak, the speed of a bird's flight, the area of a pond, all involve mathematics, while the emotions aroused by the animals may find an outlet in verse, some of which is published in the park's quarterly newsletter. An 11-year-old girl began her poem:

The snake rustles in the bushes;
Its dark eyes like radar scan the jungle,
Then there is silence.
The snake's head and nostrils work together,
Finding traces of its precious prey.

Others express their reactions in letters to the editor: 'My friend and I thought the guinea-pigs, especially the baby ones, were lovely', wrote a girl from a school on the outskirts of Birmingham, showing that it is not necessarily the exotic and bizarre that leave the greatest impression.

The central area of a wild-life park is usually made as attractive as possible by beds of flowers, a tradition perhaps started by Bristol Zoo. At Windsor there is a garden to which elderly visitors can retire and rest among a wealth of roses. Sometimes nature takes a hand; where the ground has been disturbed by sinking the wires of a boundary fence, a profusion of foxgloves may appear to offset it. But safari parks cannot make a profit on educational programmes and rose bushes: there must be special attractions. At Windsor the killer whale has been the *pièce de resistance* with its leap clear of the pool and resultant belly-flop as the climax of the show in the dolphinarium. At Blair Drummond a launch plies up and down the little loch, accompanied by sea-lions which jump for pieces of fish, and allows a close view of the wooded island where

the chimpanzees live. Elsewhere interest is maintained by introducing new animals, never before seen at large in Britain.

This provokes teasing questions: is the safari park, the ingenious
counterfeit of the African game reserve, to be accepted as an
essential ingredient in the entertainment of mobile late-twentieth-
century Britons? Can standards acceptable to the Federation of
Zoological Gardens be maintained in the proliferation of new
ventures? Do the parks really serve a conservation purpose or are
they bound to make greater and greater inroads on dwindling wild
populations of the more spectacular animals? There are already
features to which many people take exception. I could do without
Alsatians slavering at the ends of their chains by the entrance to a
jungle drive, and it was incongruous to find 'Animals Magazine',
which is campaigning strongly against the trade in skins of the big
cats, on sale in an Africana shop with a leopard skin stretched
behind the counter.

Leaving pseudo-Africa for the moment, is there a case for a
national collection of British wild life? The Nature Conservancy,
Forestry Commission and National Trust for Scotland have all
nibbled at this one, the nearest approach to which is Philip
Wayre's European assembly at Great Witchingham in Norfolk.
And what about vanishing breeds of domestic animals? The
Cotswold Farm Park at Guiting Power is 'a serious attempt to
preserve breeds of farm animals which are now facing extinction'.

I can go all the way where farm stock are concerned but find it
difficult to make up my mind on the major wild-life issue. As a
naturalist I recoil from animals in confinement, yet there is plenty
of evidence that they do not share our feelings about them: a well-
fed lion is just as happy on the grass at Longleat as on the plains
of Serengeti. I can understand the excitement of being the first
to breed a species in captivity, especially when this may lead to its
reinstatement in the wild. Birds of prey worry me, though I am
assured that a full crop compensates for idle pinions. The dolphins
doing their tricks are a great improvement on the whip-cracking
domination of the old-time circus.

The import of rare animals is now legally controlled, but it is still as easy for anyone to open a zoo as to get planning permission for a garage. It is not by the front runners that we must judge, but by their imitators. If I felt legislation was necessary in 1969, how much more so is this true today.